ROBERT ALAN SPANNER

WHO OWNS INNOVATION?

The Rights and Obligations of Employers and Employees

DOW JONES-IRWIN   Homewood, Illinois 60430

This publication is designed to provide accurate and
authoritative information in regard to the subject matter
covered. It is sold with the understanding that the
publisher is not engaged in rendering legal, accounting, or
other professional service. If legal advice or other expert
assistance is required, the services of a competent
professional person should be sought.

*From a Declaration of Principles jointly adopted by a Committee
of the American Bar Association and a Committee of Publishers.*

ISBN 0-87094-440-1

Library of Congress Catalog Card No. 84–71300

Printed in the United States of America

1 2 3 4 5 6 7 8 9 0 B 10 9 8 7 6 5 4

WHO OWNS INNOVATION?

The Rights and
Obligations
of Employers and
Employees

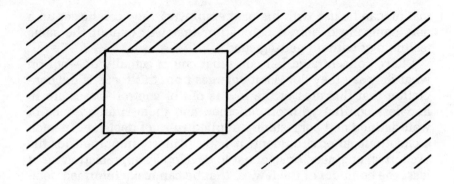

Preface

Most of the time people can live quite nicely without a detailed understanding of the law. However, when a society undergoes rapid change, old assumptions no longer work, and evolving legal doctrines must be clearly communicated. We are living in such a period of rapid—some might say tumultuous—transformation. The coming of the "information society" has been trumpeted so frequently that we may safely assume it has arrived. This brings with it a new form of "property"—information in all its protean forms—and all the unfamiliar rights, duties, and obligations associated with it.

Although large corporations in the high technology sector have developed a sophisticated understanding of proprietary information issues, many managers and technology professionals, especially in smaller corporations, have not. In less technology-intensive industries, even larger companies are frequently not completely informed about their rights regarding confidential technical and business information. It is to these sectors of the economy that this book is directed.

The scope of protectable proprietary or confidential business information is broader than most people realize. It is not just secret formulas and processes; it can be as mundane as customer data and personnel information, or as intangible as theories and ideas. The manager or employee untutored in the complexities of the law in this area may be in for a nasty shock sometime down the road. If a top employee leaves a company, what information can he use with his next employer? How can he set up a new company or join a competitor that will exploit the same technology without getting sued?

I have concentrated here on what courts actually do—not on what they say they do. What emerges from this focus is the conviction that this area of the law is out of control—cases are in hopeless conflict with one another, and there is an absence of well-defined and consistently applied rules of decision. In such a chaotic legal environment, it is particularly important for the executive, engineer, or scientist to develop an appreciation for at least the contours of the law, so that he can make informed decisions as to when he or his company are exposed to risk. Furthermore, he must be able to adopt cost-effective risk minimization strategies to deal with such risk once it has been identified.

It is easy to become cynical about an area of law that is in such disarray; an uneven application of the law violates our long-cherished view of ourselves as a nation of laws, not of men. But we must never as a society stop demanding consistency from our judicial system. Accordingly, instead of cynicism I would hope that this book might promote a public determination to bring order and systematic rules of decision to proprietary information law. If money had been treated in the medieval legal system in the same haphazard way that information is now treated, capitalism might never have gotten off the ground. It is time to get our house in order.

In writing *Who Owns Innovation?* I have called on the knowledge and experience of a number of people, whose contributions are gratefully acknowledged. Special thanks go to Jack Watson of Long & Aldridge in Atlanta, a comrade-in-arms who graciously agreed to review the manuscript despite numerous other commitments; to John Poggi, General Counsel of Spectra-Physics, who dedicated an unconscionable number of hours to reviewing and commenting on the manuscript, to the general improvement of the final product; to John O'Loughlin, Intel's Security Manager, whose advice was as savvy as he was congenial; and to Paul J. Winters, Manager of Patents and Licenses at National Semiconductor, Thomas W. Armstrong, General Counsel of Advanced Micro Devices, and Ron Reiling, Corporate Counsel of Digital Equipment Corporation, each of whom contributed helpful suggestions as well as encouraging words. And acknowledgments would not be complete without mentioning my colleagues, Arne Wagner and Cynthia Waters Verges, to whom fell the unenviable task of checking every case description and every quotation for accuracy.

On a personal level, my appreciation goes out especially to Dr. Mary Anne Edwards, who was very understanding about weekends in the library. To Susan Jelonek goes my heartfelt appreciation for her general encouragement and kind words.

Robert A. Spanner

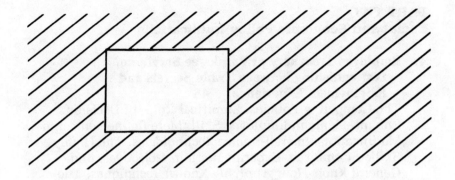

Contents

PART ONE

Overview of Trade Secrets

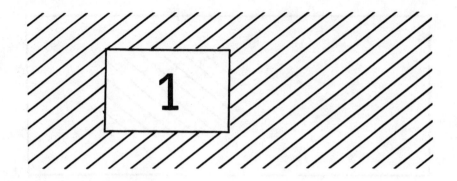

Knowledge Is Power;
Information Is Money

For several millennia mankind led a nomadic existence, hunting, gathering, and generally living by his wits. Then he domesticated the animals and planted the earth, and land became the basis of wealth and power. But with the coming of the Industrial Revolution, when a small plot of land could yield tremendous output and wealth through the concentrated application of equipment and labor, capital became the foundation of wealth and power in the economy. Now, as we all know, we are in transition to a fourth economic order, based on information in all its protean forms. We have come full circle—we are back to living by our wits.

As children, we all heard that time-worn adage "knowledge is power." It now has its counterpart in the more crass but probably more accurate epigram, "information is money." Today a person absolutely devoid of capital who has a new product idea, knowledge of the technology to execute it, the experience to manage a new venture, and the ability to persuade a venture capitalist of all the above has all the capital he needs. At the same time, a well-capitalized company with plenty of land, money, plant and equipment but an obsolete technology stands on the brink of financial ruin.

Information—sometimes referred to as "human capital," to use the term coined by economist Gary Becker two decades ago—is the new wealth. That aggregate of education, training, knowledge, and experience is in the process of supplanting capital as the principal source of economic value, just as capital supplanted land centuries ago. Social institutions will have to adapt to respond to this economic metamorphosis, and none more so than the law.

As will become evident in the following pages, courts have struggled with cases involving rights in information. They have often tried to apply traditional property concepts to information, despite the fact that information often has no tangible form, and can be simultaneously "possessed" by many people. Not surprisingly, the results have not been satisfactory. The decisions are in hopeless conflict with one another, and the rationales offered for the rulings are frequently unpersuasive or wholly absent. Trade secret law—the body of common law dealing with information issues—is in disarray.

This situation will become intolerable as information-based economic activity continues to grow in importance. Companies need to know, with some degree of certainty, whether they have a proprietary technology before they spend millions to exploit it. Employees, entrepreneurs, and their venture capital partners need to know with some assurance what information in the employee's possession can and can't be used in a new venture. Firms that want to recruit a key employee away from a competitor need to know what their prospects are if they get sued. In short, firms need *answers*, not vague precepts and doctrines that can be applied in inconsistent ways and which provide no basis for planning.

Only one class of people benefit from the uncertainty inhering in trade secret law—the lawyers who advise on such matters. Lawyers thrive in uncertainty—it provides an opportunity for the full exercise of their creative talents. Strategy has become all-important in trade secret cases—as the contents of this book will readily attest.

But providing employment and income to lawyers, while certainly a laudable goal, is probably not an adequate social justification for leaving trade secret law in the state of confusion it is presently in. And it is not just a question of the law not being responsive to the needs of a changing economy. We have always prided ourselves on being a nation of laws, not of men. The American ideal dictates that like-situated persons be treated similarly. When, for whatever reason, that does not happen, it is perceived to be "unfair," and this perception breeds disrespect for the rule of law.

No one can reasonably expect mathematical precision from general principles of law, but it is not unreasonable for companies and their employees to expect more guidance from trade secret law as to their respective rights and obligations than the law is presently able to provide.

How to Use This Book

Trade secret law is essentially a story about lawsuits—lots of them, brought all over the country. The best way to explore this area of law is to start where the courts start in resolving trade secret cases—with the rules defining what a trade secret is supposed to consist of and when a trade secret has been unlawfully taken. Chapter 2 contains a brief introduction to these legal notions.

Chapter 2 concludes with an explanation of the dynamics of trade secret litigation. It explains why trade secret litigation can be so onerous for the parties, for their lawyers, and for the judge hearing the case. Much of the strategic discussion throughout this book is directed to the avoidance of litigation; this chapter explains why that is such a worthy objective.

As companies came to recognize the commercial value of more and more categories of information, the demand for more extensive restrictions on the use of company information by employees has inevitably followed. The courts have obligingly added to what has traditionally been regarded as trade secret subject matter. Some will be pleasantly surprised to learn how broadly the concept of a trade secret has come to be interpreted, while others may be horrified. For example, machine designs and processes have long been regarded as protectable technical secrets, but how many people are aware that data, technical evaluations, and even theories and ideas have from time to time received the trade secret mantle, and that employees have been prohibited from using such embodiments of information in subsequent employment? Even methodologies for the organization and processing of information have sometimes been treated as trade secrets. And what about software? Can the marriage of common programming skills with concepts common in the industry to which the software relates result in something "secret"?

Chapter 3 deals with these issues and many more; it is a compendium of the most important types of information for which trade secret protection has been claimed. Almost everyone will be interested in something discussed in this chapter, but few will be interested in everything it contains. The reader should let his interests be his guide.

Perhaps the most intransigent problem in trade secret law today is differentiating between proprietary information, which a company's employees may not utilize after terminating their employment, and an employee's general knowledge and experience, which he is completely free to use for his own purposes. For example, if an employee, after comprehensive training and considerable on-the-job experience, acquires the capability to develop something or perform some task, which ability is not widely available in the industry, does the knowledge "belong" to the employer or to the employee? Or contrarily, if an employee is hired because he possesses a special expertise, and through the application of that expertise creates certain innovations, may the information embodied in the innovations be freely used by the employee, or is it company proprietary information? And what about knowledge of research objectives, or experimental results, or just plain old "know-how"—can these be company trade secrets? The courts have struggled with these and related issues, and a review of that struggle appears in Chapter 4.

Chapter 5 explores a related—and equally difficult—issue: how innovative does an innovation have to be to qualify for trade secret protection? To illustrate the dilemma, consider a refinement in a well-known process, or a modification to a familiar machine, leading to improved performance. Do such improvements partake of the public nature of the devices and processes to which they pertain, or are they sufficiently "novel" to warrant legal protection against unauthorized use? A similar question arises with respect to alleged trade secrets which are mere combinations of common components. If the aggregate of such components, however, is not common, and results in superior commercial or technical performance, is that enough to qualify the combination as something worth protecting?

Such questions can become almost metaphysical; but with Chapters 6 and 7 we turn to more practical matters. The essence of a trade secret, according to the conventional wisdom, is secrecy in fact; the cases often recite that trade secrets must be secret. That proposition is critically analyzed in Chapter 6.

The primary purpose of security is not to insure legal protection at any rate; it is to keep proprietary information from leaving the premises. How that can best be achieved is set forth in

Chapter 6. In particular, common mistakes are identified so that unintended loss of legal protection can be avoided.

Preserving the secrecy of proprietary information has two aspects: (1) keeping such information out of the wrong hands, and (2) keeping information in the right hands from being disclosed. The first facet is a matter of *security;* the second, a matter of *confidentiality.* The central instrument in maintaining confidentiality is the employee confidentiality and invention assignment agreement. This agreement is analyzed in detail in Chapter 7. Numerous legal issues are implicated by the terms of such an agreement, and they are identified so that companies, as well as their employees, can take appropriate defensive measures.

When a key employee contemplates leaving his employment, either to start his own business or to join a competitor, how he conducts himself thenceforth will be of critical importance, not only to himself but to his subsequent employer as well. He must be vigilant to avoid not only a trade secret dispute, but also a claim of employee disloyalty as well. For example, extreme care must be taken in communications with colleagues and customers not to overstep the bounds of legal propriety. And of course an employee intending to join the competition must learn what he is required to tell his employer regarding his future plans. These issues are addressed in Chapter 8.

It is the best of times, because opportunity is never greater than in a society in transition; and it is the worst of times, because never has competition been more intense. Just a small competitive advantage can make a huge difference in these circumstances. Perhaps the knowledge derived from this book can contribute in some small measure to securing that competitive edge, and lead on to fame and fortune. For be they good times or bad, it is certainly the most exciting and tumultuous of times, and to believe that almost anything is possible is simply to have a realistic appraisal of the situation.

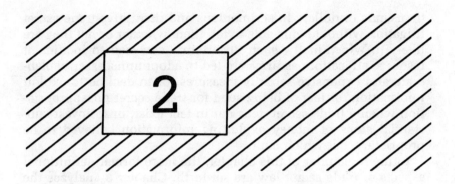

2

What's It All about

This book is about two categories of knowledge: *trade secrets* and *confidential business information*. Confidential information is operationally defined as business information that is confidential, but is not a trade secret; so let us first consider the nature of a trade secret.

A trade secret can be defined in three ways: judicially, operationally, and pragmatically. The judicial definition of a trade secret raises more questions than it answers. And the operational definition is hardly more enlightening, consisting of little more than an enumeration of the factors which courts utilize in deciding what kinds of information are protectable trade secrets.

The pragmatic definition of a trade secret is that which a judge says it is. This perspective is saved from cynicism by the fact that there is little agreement among lawyers, judges, and legal scholars as to just what should be regarded as a trade secret and under what circumstances it should be protected, and saying a trade secret is merely what a given court says it is is not so far from the truth. Indeed, it is not uncommon for two courts to apply the same legal principles to similar facts and arrive at precisely the opposite conclusions.

This want of predictability is wearing on everyone, because the ability to plan is impossibly compromised. Such a state of affairs also makes things difficult for lawyers, who must advise their clients whether or not to spend tens or hundreds of thousands of dollars in acrimonious and disruptive trade secret litigation without being able to tell them whether or not they are likely to win. Finally, such uncertainty can lead to inefficient resource allocation, as firms are led to adopt unnecessarily elaborate and expensive security measures, or to decline to exploit information for fear of being sued for trade secret misappropriation when a trade secret does not in fact exist, or to invest substantial sums of money exploiting information believed to be proprietary, but which isn't.

In the remainder of this chapter, the more formal definitional aspects of trade secret law are set forth. Chapter 3 analyzes the kinds of information that have actually been accorded legal protection.

Basic Definitions

The most commonly quoted definition of a trade secret was adopted several decades ago by a group of legal scholars in a treatise entitled the *Restatement of Torts:*

> A trade secret may consist of any formula, pattern, device or compilation of information which is used in one's business, and which gives him an opportunity to obtain an advantage over competitors who do not know or use it. It may be a formula for a chemical compound, a process of manufacturing, treating or preserving materials, a pattern for a machine or other device, or a list of customers. It differs from other secret information in a business in that it is not simply information as to single or ephemeral events in the conduct of the business, as, for example, the amount or other terms of a secret bid for a contract or the salary of certain employees, or the security investments made or contemplated, or the date fixed for the announcement of a new policy or for bringing out a new model or the like. A trade secret is a process or device for continuous use in the operation of the business. Generally it relates to the production of goods, as, for example, a machine or formula for the production of an article. It may, however, relate to the sale of goods or to other operations in the business, such as a code for determining discounts, rebates or other concessions in a price list or catalogue, or a list of specialized customers, or a method of bookkeeping or other office management.

Another definition in currency is that contained in the Uniform Trade Secrets Act, which has been adopted or is under consideration in a number of states:

"Trade secret" means information, including a formula, pattern, compilation, program, device, method, technique, or process, that:
(i) derives independent economic value, actual or potential, from not being generally known to, and not being readily ascertainable by proper means by, other persons who can obtain economic value from its disclosure or use, and
(ii) is the subject of efforts that are reasonable under the circumstances to maintain its secrecy.

A majority of states and federal courts conceive of a trade secret as a form of property, which is "taken" when one uses or discloses the secret to another without authorization. But another approach many courts follow is to focus not on the nature of what is taken, but instead on the legal duty owed by one to whom a trade secret has been disclosed not to use or disclose it without authorization. To put this difference in perspective, one might analogize trade secret misappropriation to trespassing. When a squatter sets himself up on someone else's property and deprives that person of the use of a portion of his land, has there been a "taking" of property (for certainly possession and use are two principal incidents of owning land)? Or does the squatter merely violate a legal duty owed to the property holder not to trespass on his land? Whether an unauthorized use or disclosure of a trade secret is conceived of as a taking of property or as a breach of a legal duty to maintain a confidence can determine the outcome of a given case. Here's why.

As will be seen in the succeeding section, trade secret litigation turns on an evaluation of a number of intangible factors rather than on the application of a specific legal doctrine to the facts presented in a particular case. Since most trade secret cases arise out of conduct that is either manifestly deceitful or at least arguably improper, focusing one's attention on whether there was a relationship of confidence existing between the parties, and, if so, whether the relationship was breached, will result in a finding of trade secret misappropriation much of the time. If, on the other hand, one starts with the inquiry whether there was even any "property" to be misappropriated in the first place, there is a decidedly different mind-set. To state it another way, the "breach of confidence" approach focuses on whether there *was* a legal violation, while the "property" approach looks first to whether there even *could* be a legal violation. In actual practice, in cases where the theft of trade secrets is primarily conceived of in terms of breach of confidence, the court often addresses whether there is trade secret subject matter only as an afterthought, if at all. If, on the other hand, a court declares the starting point to be not whether there was a breach of confidence but whether there was even a trade secret to take, then there is usually a much more detailed analysis of the prerequisites for trade secret protection—often resulting in the conclusion that one or more of them are missing.

An Operational Definition

The legal definition set forth in the Restatement is more a definition by example than a precise formulation of a legal rule. The Restatement does go on, however, to enumerate several factors to be evaluated in the determination of what constitutes a trade secret:

1. The extent to which the information is known outside of the business.
2. The extent to which the information is known by those involved in the business.
3. The nature and extent of measures taken to protect the secrecy of the information.
4. The value of the information.
5. The amount of time, effort, and money expended in developing the information.
6. The degree of difficulty with which the information could be properly acquired or duplicated by others.

Although these six enumerated indicia of trade secrecy are not usually applied lockstep by the courts, they have played a prominent role in trade secret litigation, and every so often courts will add new factors to be considered. For example, in one case where the issue presented was whether a customer list was a trade secret, the court stated it would also assess: (a) the extent to which the relationship between the employer and employee was confidential, (b) the method by which the employee acquired or compiled the list, (c) the employee's relationship with his customers, and (d) whether the employee gained an unfair advantage from use of the list.

It is this "factor analysis" that leads trade secret decisions into hopeless conflict with each other. Since there is no firm and fixed definition of a trade secret and courts are applying different considerations of varying priorities, it should not be surprising that similar circumstances are distinguished from each other by judicial distinctions one judge characterized as "shaded into each other by lines so fine that it is doubtful whether anything but a nice sense of honor can keep them distinguished."

The Real-World Definition of a Trade Secret

The pragmatist defines a trade secret as that which the courts say it is. Rather than applying legal theories or an analysis of factors to determine what kinds of subject matter are protectable trade secrets, the pragmatist is result oriented, and assumes that what courts have held to be trade secrets in the past will be held to be trade secrets in the future. This approach is neither more nor less successful a predictor of how a case will be resolved than more analytical approaches.

Trade Secret Misappropriation Defined

Assuming that one can identify a trade secret, the next question is under what circumstances use or disclosure of that information will be considered wrongful. There are two principal circumstances giving rise to liability for misuse of a trade secret:

1. Where the information was communicated confidentially to someone and that person disclosed or used the information in breach of that confidence.
2. Where the information was discovered by improper means.

There are many circumstances in which the disclosure of business information is considered to be in confidence. One example, of course, is an express agreement by the person receiving the information to keep it secret and not to use it without authorization. Such express agreements are often found in contracts for the license of a device or process. But there need not be an express agreement for a confidence to arise, for the law *implies* a condition of confidence in certain commercial relationships. The most common of these is the employer-employee relationship. A disclosure of trade secrets to an employee is generally assumed by the law to be in confidence, whether there is an express agreement to that effect or not, and the employee may not later use those secrets in the service of another employer. Another example of a disclosure presumed to be in confidence is information communicated from one partner in a joint venture to the other. Usually trade secret cases involve a ᴊreach of confidence of some kind, and usually the confidential relationship involved is the employer-employee relationship.

A less frequent form of trade secret misappropriation involves acquisition of trade secret information by improper means. Breaking and entering would certainly be deemed an improper means of procuring information, as would fraudulent inducement. The Uniform Trade Secrets Act lists a number of "improper means" of obtaining information, including theft, bribery, misrepresentation, inducing breach of confidence, and espionage.

Confidential Business Information Defined

As the Restatement definition of trade secrets indicates, only information that is in continuoᴜs use in the operation of a business is supposed to qualify as a trade secret. As the cases discussed in this book indicate, this rule is often honored more in the breach than in the observance. But at any rate, there will still be innumerable items of information which, though not in continuous use—and perhaps not even "in use" at all—are highly confidential and would be of imme surable benefit in the hands of a competitor. The Restatement lists such things as contract bids, the date of new product announcements, and investments. In addition, such personnel information as salary, benefits, and level of job satisfaction would be of inestimable value to a competitor seeking to recruit a company's key employees, but is not information in continuous "use." Similarly, knowledge of a company's expansion plans or anticipated R&D would be of critical interest to a competitor, and would ordinarily be kept confidential. Confidential business information may relate to single events, to future events, or to assessments and appraisals.

Breach of Fiduciary Duty Defined

When a company hires an employee, certain reciprocal obligations are implied. For example, the employee implicitly understands that he must be present for a prescribed period of time and will be subject to the direction of his superiors. The employer understands that he must make regular payments of salary, maintain a safe working environment, and so on. There is one other obligation which inheres in the employment relationship—the employee's fiduciary obligation, or duty of loyalty. The law requires an employee not to act in a manner contrary to the commercial interests of his employer. If he does, he is said to be in breach of his ficuciary duty.

A Brief Explanation of Legal Nomenclature and Procedure

To anyone who has had even a passing encounter with a lawsuit, most of this section may seem elementary. It is included for completeness and may be referred to when the terms or procedures referred to throughout this book confuse or mystify.

Many areas of law are based on specific statutory enactments, such as securities law, antitrust law, and criminal law. But for the most part, the law of trade secrets is not based on statutes; it is court-made case law built up over many decades. Trade secret law is thus part of the *common law*, which is predicated on the tradition that decisions rendered in past cases control the outcome of future cases. This is changing somewhat with the promulgation of the Uniform Trade Secrets Act, a statute that represents an effort to bring together the best of the common-law rules of decision adopted in the various states and to make them uniform throughout the country. But even the Uniform Trade Secrets Act is itself a creature of the common law. For all intents and purposes, trade secret law remains part of the common-law tradition.

The common law of each state is theoretically independent from all of the others, just as each state has its own set of statutes. Therefore, there could theoretically be 50 separate versions of trade secret law. But as a practical matter, state courts rely on the trade secret decisions of sister jurisdictions almost as much as their own.

Violations of legal duties recognized by the common law are called *torts*. Trespass is a tort; so is fraud, defamation, and negligence. In like manner, trade secret misappropriation and breach of confidence are torts, for the law implies a duty not to disclose information acquired in confidence and not to obtain information by improper means. Torts give rise to a private right of action (i.e., the right to bring a lawsuit), but a tort is not punishable as a crime unless it has been made a crime by statute. For example, assault is a tort and a crime. Many states have passed laws making the misappropriation of trade secrets a crime under certain specified circumstances.

When an individual or company believes his proprietary information has been improperly taken or used by some other person or entity and institutes a lawsuit, he (or it) becomes the *plaintiff*. The plaintiff is the person or entity initiating the lawsuit. The parties against whom the lawsuit is brought are all called *defendants*.

In a lawsuit there are two principal types of relief available: (1) damages, and (2) an injunction. Damages means money awarded to compensate the plaintiff for losses the plaintiff can show he sustained on account of the defendants' wrongful conduct. An injunction is a court order to the defendants to stop doing something; it is enforceable by sanctions for contempt of court, including fines and imprisonment. Various types of injunctions have been awarded in trade secret cases, including injunctions against use or disclosure of trade secret information, injunctions against use of processes or devices utilizing trade secret information, injunctions against hiring an employee in possession of trade secret information, and injunctions against competition entirely. Injunctions are usually issued for only a limited period of time, the duration of which depends on the facts of each case.

In trade secret cases more frequently than in most other types of cases, the defendant's conduct causes injury to the plaintiff that cannot be compensated for by damages. For example, a trade secret resulting from long research and development may have been misappropriated by a competitor who is undercutting the plaintiff's price because his R&D expenditures don't have to be amortized. By the time the case gets to trial—which may be years after the plaintiff initiates the lawsuit—the plaintiff may have been driven out of business, or the competitor may have already disclosed the trade secret to others, which would destroy its value forever. In such circumstances, the plaintiff may, and usually does, seek a *preliminary injunction*, which is an injunction issued during the pendency of the lawsuit. To obtain a preliminary injunction, the plaintiff must meet rigorous requirements, including a demonstration that he will probably prevail at trial and that he cannot be compensated in damages for his loss.

After a trade secret case commences, both sides will conduct *discovery*, a process by which each side tries to determine the facts. Each side can send written questions to the other (interrogatories), which must be answered under oath, and can direct that certain documents be produced for inspection and copying. In addition, each side will usually take *depositions*. A deposition is a procedure whereby a witness is ordered to appear at a certain date and time to answer questions under oath, and the questions and answers are taken down by a court reporter for later use in the proceedings. A transcript of the deposition is prepared by the court reporter and is made available to all parties.

If the plaintiff seeks a preliminary injunction and loses, there is a tendency on the part of trade secret plaintiffs (and their lawyers) to throw in the towel and either dismiss the case or settle it on unfavorable terms, rather than take the case to trial. This is regrettable. Losing a preliminary injunction hearing means no more than failing to demonstrate one or more of the prerequisites for injunctive relief. For example, if the court believes that the plaintiff will recover substantial damages at trial, which will fully compensate him for his losses, the judge must deny a motion for a preliminary injunction; but such denial obviously does not mean that the case has no merit. Moreover, a judge's perspective of a case during the preliminary injunction hearing may differ substantially from the perspective gained by the jury in a well-prepared and well-executed trial. These two segments of a trade secret case should be regarded as separate productions, rather than as scenes in the same drama. At trial, a trade secret case takes on a life of its own, and the trial will often bear little resemblance to what has gone before.

Epilogue: A View from the Trenches

The foregoing is an abbreviated description of the framework within which trade secret litigation occurs. But no chapter entitled "What's It All about" would be complete without putting some flesh and blood on this legal skeleton by discussing some of the realities of trade secret litigation.

Trade secret actions are usually not fun to participate in. Such litigation, between companies of any size, bears a certain resemblance to Dante's descent into the rings of Hell, and any company that has been through one feels like Georgia after Sherman. There are many reasons why such litigation so resembles warfare, such as the extreme threat that loss of a trade secret poses to the profitability of a company, the fact that these suits are between former colleagues and friends, the peril that such a lawsuit poses to the continued existence of a start-up, the disruption of operations that results, and the burden high attorneys' fees place upon all parties. Magnifying all these factors tenfold is the fact that what would ordinarily be done over the course of two or three years must be accomplished in two or three months, in preparation for the preliminary injunction hearing.

Here is what typically happens. First a swarm of the company's own attorneys will descend on the company (they travel in groups because there is too much for one lawyer to do in the short amount of time available). They will slow operations to a crawl, first by taking every piece of paper out of the files, off the walls, and away from the plant floor to copy, and then by interviewing anything that moves. Thereafter, even though all the paper has been replaced, no one seems able to find *anything;* and everyone who has been interrogated begins to wonder whether he too is under suspicion, or whether he might have erred and prejudiced the company's litigation prospects.

Then the lawyers review their findings with management, and all the mistakes, misunderstandings, indifference, and ill-advised policies of the past five years or so are suddenly exposed to view all at once in one great cathartic spasm, to the dismay and horror of almost everyone. The lawyers and management try to forge some plausible explanation for what has been allowed to happen, but a thick gloom sets in that won't be dispelled until the equally glaring foul-ups of the opponents have been disclosed.

Depositions will begin next, and many of the company's key personnel will be incapacitated for weeks with deposition preparation, deposition attendance, and strategy sessions. Even when they aren't directly engaged in the prosecution of the lawsuit, they will be thinking about it, for the sense of urgency that pervades trade secret litigation as a result of the acute time constraints is inevitably communicated to the participants and catches them up in its web of consequence and tension.

The depositions themselves ruin everyone's schedule and disposition. Taken under oath, testimony gained in depositions is customarily used in lieu of live examination at the preliminary injunction hearing. The strain of concentrating for hours on end and days at a time to avoid making a damaging admission, and trying to accurately remember events occurring some time earlier, is debilitating, as is the prospect of being cross-examined *ad infinitum* by an incredulous lawyer with an unerring instinct for the most trivial detail.

After the depositions comes the final preparation of legal memoranda, the drafting of applicants, the marking of documents as exhibits, and endless meetings to decide what to present and how to anticipate and rebut the opposition's arguments.

Here is how one federal court judge described a trade secret action pending before him:

> This case, which at its inception involved issues of no great complexity, has become a gigantic, grotesque monster of procedural strife which is about to consume the parties and the court unless it can be brought under some control. During the year and a half in which this case has been pending, both parties have engaged in aggressive, abusive, and harrassing discovery...the court has been inundated with every conceivable type of motion, and nearly every ruling of the court has been met with objections and motions for reconsideration. As a result, this court cannot but feel that the parties are more anxious to bring about the financial collapse of their opposition than to move this case toward final resolution.

With so much headache and expense at stake, the homily about an ounce of prevention takes on added significance concerning trade secret litigation. It is always true that the best trade secret case is the one that was so good it never had to be brought. Trade secret litigation can be won before it happens, through careful planning and the will to persevere.

What Information Is Protectable?

As the following pages demonstrate, the concepts of "trade secrets" and "confidential business information" are almost limitless in their potential scope. Virtually anything that can be said to embody information can qualify, and some of the categories of information that have received judicial recognition as trade secrets may surprise (or appall) the discerning reader.

Trade secret subject matter (throughout this book the term "trade secrets" if often used as a shorthand designation for all forms of confidential information in the business context) consists either of technical information or business information. "Technical" trade secrets will be considered first.

Scientific and Technological Secrets

In the uncertain universe of trade secret law, one of the few verities that can be asserted is that devices and machinery, processes and methods of manufacture, and formulations and compositions of matter all constitute recognized trade secret subject matter. In cases involving these categories of information, trade secret protection may not have been afforded because of such factors as the lack of adequate security procedures, voluntary disclosures by the purported trade secret owner, and the availability of the alleged trade secret information in the public domain; but the suitability of trade secret protection in the first place has not been an issue.

Since there is little debate regarding the legal protectability of devices, processes, and formulations, let us turn our attention to more problematic areas.

Pure Information: Data, Theories, and Ideas

1. **Data:** Given the readiness with which courts assume the protectability of processes, devices, and formulations, one might reasonably assume that data relating to these three categories of information would also be protectable. After all, it is only a small step from plans and blueprints, or from chemical formulas, to performance data and R&D analyses. And this is indeed what one seems to find. Illustrative of the legal protection afforded to pure data is an Ohio case brought by an ozone equipment manufacturer. When one of its key employees wished to accept the presidency of a competitor, the company sought to enjoin the employee from doing so. It argued that, among other things, he was generally acquainted with the operating performance data for the company's ozone generators, and that he was familiar with R&D reports evaluating the company's equipment and the potential uses to which ozone could be put. Finding such data to be proprietary to the company, the court enjoined the employee from joining the competitor for one year. Similarly, a court in another case ruled that the data generated from experimentation on the plastic incorporated into the rollers used in film processing equipment also constituted a trade secret.

Tolerance data is also commonly protected. Even for publicly marketed articles, where everything else about the design may be readily ascertainable by any competitor, tolerances will not be. As every design engineer knows, tolerance data can be almost as important as specifications.

To achieve trade secret protection, data need not be so closely related to the operational attributes of a device or process. For example, in one decision, *Tlapek v. Chevron Oil Company*, a Chevron Oil employee had utilized a company's geophysical data to develop a theory to predict the existence of oil in a certain geological formation in Arkansas. After unsuccessfully urging the company to drill in the region, the employee resigned and started buying up oil leases himself. But the court ordered the employee to turn over the leases to his former employer on the ground that he had exploited Chevron's trade secret geophysical data to discover this oil exploration opportunity.

2. **Technical assessments:** Even mere qualitative assessments have sometimes been protected as a trade secret. For example, a manufacturer of heating furnaces sued a rival who had hired away one of its employees and then began selling a similarly constructed furnance. The rival company defended by asserting that all the attributes of the furnace had been disclosed when the furnace was sold to the public and therefore, no feature of the furnace was secret. But the trial judge ruled that even if the features of the furnace itself had been disclosed, this was not the case for certain other information in the employee's possession, relating to the economic efficiencies and engineering benefits attributable to the method of construction—such as the fact that using screws instead of welds was less expensive, or that a certain design change reduced stress and cracking. Such information was deemed protectable as a trade secret. Similarly, a Pennsylvania court found a mere "appreciation" of technical problems on the part of a company vice president to be confidential and imposed an injunction against competitive employment in a similar position. Even though the company was using a proven and well-known technology—the injection of pressurized nitrogen into oil wells to increase productivity—the judge found that an appreciation of the technical problems and necessary safety precautions associated with the use of this technology was information which could be regarded as proprietary to the company. But another court has expressed the view that an appreciation of technological attributes is a mere "emotion or feeling [that] cannot be appropriated and cannot be a trade secret."

3. **Theories and ideas:** Even theories and ideas have been drawn under the trade secret umbrella. In the Chevron case mentioned above, the court stated that even if Chevron's employee had not utilized confidential company information to develop his theory, the theory *itself* was confidential business information belonging to Chevron that the employee was not permitted to use for his own purposes. Similarly, in a case brought by a tennis ball throwing machine manufacturer, the trial judge held that a director's idea for a smaller, improved machine was a trade secret belonging to the company, which the originator could not utilize—even though the company did not show any enthusiasm

for the idea and even though the company had no plans to utilize the idea in the future.

Extending trade secret protection to such intangible embodiments of information as theories, ideas, and even appreciations has obvious implications for the mobility of executives, scientists, and engineers, as well as for new venture formation. A few courts, recognizing the potential problems, have declined the opportunity to adopt so expansive an interpretation of trade secrets. For example, one court has flatly ruled that a theory cannot be a trade secret because it lacks "form and substance."

4. **Organization of information:** The same inconsistency is found in the treatment of systems for organizing information. The management information system of an outside vendor was held to be a trade secret in one case where the defendant's own employees testified to its value. But another case held that a management information system developed by an employee was *not* a trade secret belonging to the company; the employee was entitled to use for himself the knowledge he gained in development of the system. Similarly, a coordinated methodology for the solution of complex problems has also been held not to be a trade secret.

Software

In trade secret law, software is the new kid on the block. A sporadic occurrence in the 1960s and 70s, trade secret cases involving computer software are likely to become a common phenomenon in this decade as the microprocessor becomes a prevalent feature of daily life.

Software has given courts trouble. Computer programs are so complicated and unintelligible on their face that it seems they *must* be valuable secrets, but for the same reasons it is difficult to identify *what* is secret and unique about them.

In only a few trade secret software cases have specific logic and processing features been identified as innovative in and of themselves. For example, in one case involving the alleged misappropriation of a controller for a computer, the court found the plaintiff's method of data flow between computer and disk to be unique, as well as its method of word addressability and the manner in which it used a buffer. But such cases are rare. In most software cases, the judge does not—or cannot—describe what *specifically* makes a computer program protectable. And this is understandable, for it would take a not inconsiderable command of computer science to appreciate algorithmic wizardry, the subtleties of input and output methodologies, the cleverness of search and access strategies, and so forth. But the absence of such a mastery has not proved an impediment to the judicial recognition of computer programs as bona fide trade secrets, following a sort of "I-know-it-when-I-see-it" reasoning. Take, for example, one case concerning certain operating system software for a time-sharing system. The judge found the software to be a trade secret, referring to the "underlying technologies and design," the "logic and coherence," the "speed, accuracy, cost, and commercial feasibility," and the "peculiar and unique accomplishments and technical skills of the developers" the software embodied. But nowhere did he actually identify what features in the programs at issue he was referring to, or how they differed from techniques well known in the trade.

Another example involved a dispute over a structural analysis program that several employees developed, then redeveloped in the service of a competitor. In a manner similar to the case previously discussed, the judge asserted that the organization of subroutines, the coding, and "other factors" constituted confidential information protected from disclosure, without explaining exactly *what* it was about the software that was confidential and proprietary or why. Indeed, in response to the assertion that the program embodied nothing more than what was already disclosed in the literature, the judge asserted that nonetheless the combination of elements in the program was unique and valuable. Why? The parties were not offered an explanation.

But what is actually going on in such software cases seems clear. The evidence demonstrated to the court that whatever was in this intellectual black box called a computer program, it was *valuable*. Thousands of hours had been spent in its development, and it commanded tens of thousands of dollars in license fees. And since it was valuable, the court seemed to think it should be protected. The purest expression of this position is embodied in a Pennsylvania decision concerning a mundane program to process subscription lists for the purpose of targeting advertising to subscribers who had recently moved. The judge acknowledged that both the concepts embodied in the program and the expertise necessary to create the software were matters of public knowledge. Yet he held the program to be a protectable trade secret anyway because of the investment of time and money to develop it and its value in the market.

There is nothing in principle wrong with considering the value of software, the cost of development, and the cost of development by a competitor in determining whether software is a trade secret, so long as the difference between software and the knowledge to develop it is kept firmly in view. A protected computer program need not have required trade secret knowledge for its development. To assume otherwise would have serious implications for the employee-programmer who developed the program using *only* common programming techniques and concepts well known in the industry to which the application relates. If trade secret protection were to be extended to anything beyond the program listing itself in such circumstances, the programmer could be prohibited from using his knowledge and experience to develop a competing product for a rival—even for a simple and straightforward application. This would be like saying that once an employee had solved a difficult math problem during the course of his employment, he could never solve that kind of problem for anyone else. Such a result would be inconsistent with the notion that an employee may not be restrained from using his personal skills along with commonly known information in the service of a competitor. (See Chapter 4.)

Let us now consider an intermediate situation, where no unique or innovative programming techniques are used, but where the program is extremely complicated and embodies many design decisions. In one California case, an employee had developed software that life insurance companies licensed for $100,000 to $200,000. The employee then joined a competitor and developed a competing program. The fact that there were significant and numerous software design alternatives led the judge to conclude that the similarities in the competing programs were not attributable simply to the use of commonly known life insurance industry concepts. Since there were numerous ways the software *could* have been written, and since the decision pathway actually chosen obviously resulted in a commercially successful product, the combination of choices actually adopted was regarded as proprietary to the programmer's employer.

Not all software cases have resulted in the finding of a protectable trade secret. In a dispute over the alleged copying of a CAD/CAM (computer-aided design and manufacturing) system for jewelry engraving, the Minnesota Supreme Court ruled that the assembly of commonly available software components into an integrated system lacked novelty. Therefore, it didn't qualify as a trade secret. The debate as to whether novelty is required for trade secret protection is a recurring one (see Chapter 5) and is not unique to software cases. With so many off-the-shelf programs coming into being, the issue of novelty may become paramount in many future cases involving "assembly" rather than independent development.

A final issue in the software context is the extent to which sale will forfeit trade secret protection. It is a truism of trade secret law that public sale of a system, device, and so on that discloses the secret loses the availability of trade secret protection. Some software vendors have tried to avoid this result by only *licensing* the software under a pledge to keep it confidential. In one case where a program had been licensed to 600 companies, trade secret status was ruled to be still intact. But the limits of this strategy are only now being tested. Whether a court would uphold a WordStar or VisiCalc as trade secrets under *any* circumstances after their mass distribution is at least problematic.

Business Information

In the course of business operations, there is much information generated that one would not ordinarily think of as trade secrets, but which companies will do everything possible to keep confidential. Personnel information is one example. Not only would the disclosure of sensitive personnel information be of invaluable assistance to competitors in recruiting the company's employees, but the company may have good reasons for not wanting even its *own* employees to have access to such information. Financial data is another category of information a company may not want its competitors, its customers, or its suppliers to know. The fact that a company is in a weakened financial condition could stimulate a competitor to launch an aggressive marketing campaign or to slash its prices in the hope of administering the coup de grace. Or a firm might not want its cost data disclosed to its competitors for fear of revealing that it has a cheaper source of supply. Other types of confidential information a firm might wish not to have revealed include competitive bids, bidding procedures, customer prices, supplier costs, new product developments, and expansion plans. The list of possibilities is endless.

Courts have been quite liberal about the types of business information they will protect against unauthorized use or disclosure. Major categories of information that have arisen repeatedly in trade secret litigation are considered in the following pages.

Customer Lists and Confidential
Customer Information

Customer lists have engendered more litigation than any other single category of information, and it is not hard to see why. Not every chemical company, for instance, will have proprietary chemical formulas, and even in such technology industries as semiconductors or lasers, only a few companies will actually have developed trade secret methods and processes. But every company—right down to one-man retail service firms—has a customer list. And particularly in service companies, where much of the firm's going concern value is wrapped up in goodwill, it is understandable why companies would be vigilant—even violent—about preventing use of their customer information by competitors.

As uncertain as trade secret litigation in other areas may be, it is a paragon of certitude compared to the vagaries of customer list litigation. Virtually every conceivable position has been taken by some court at some time. There is little agreement as to outcome, legal theory, or even the proper social policies to be furthered—not just between jurisdictions but within them. One Texas appellate court accurately described customer list cases as a "trade secret quagmire," and acerbically observed: "In the numerous decisions in this area will be found language which at least tends to support each of the following statements: (1) Practically all customer lists will be protected; (2) Practically no such list will be protected; (3) Only written lists will be protected; (4) Only lists of retail customers will be protected. . . ." And that court concluded: "There is no reliable test for determining when a list is secret, nor is there agreement as to the type of customer information which will be considered confidential."

In a few states where there have been a large volume of customer list cases, one can guess with some degree of accuracy the likely outcome of a given case simply by comparing its facts with those of previous cases. But in other jurisdictions, customer list litigation can resemble Las Vegas more than law. It is often next to impossible to predict which one of a number of competing principles, policies, and rationales a given judge will find most compelling in a given set of circumstances.

In the few pages available here, it would be impossible to set down definitively the customer list law of each jurisdiction—or of any jurisdiction—and it would be equally difficult to set forth any definitive rules of decision, since there aren't any. But the most commonly presented issues can at least be identified, and their resolution by a representative sample of courts illustrated.

The reason for conferring legal protection on customers lists is that it is perceived to be inequitable to allow an employee to deprive his former employer of the patronage of customers it took considerable time, effort and money to identify. Therefore, there is general agreement that lists of customers are protectable only if the identity of customers is not readily ascertainable by reference to publicly available sources; otherwise, no substantial expenditure of time and money would have been involved in developing the list. The argument is usually about what constitutes reasonable ascertainability. For example, if some of the customers' identities are available from public sources and some are not, is the customer list as a whole protectable? A few courts have answered that question in the affirmative.

Another issue is whether customer identities are readily ascertainable if they are not available from such publicly accessible sources as the telephone book or industry directories, but the identities are not "secret" either, in the sense that sales or delivery personnel could be followed and the identities of a company's customers readily ascertained by this kind of "espionage." Can a former employee who serviced a customer list of this type be prevented from soliciting the customers after his employment terminates? Resolution of this question has turned on what might charitably be termed some mighty fine distinctions. For example, two cases in Pennsylvania came to directly opposite conclusions. In one case the employees drove well-marked trucks, while in the other they drove personal automobiles. And a California court found a difference between a list of customers who had ice delivered to them and the identity of customers who bought ice off the dock.

Customer lists are most often found to be protectable trade secrets in the context of home delivery operations or sales to a delimited portion of the retail consuming public. The reason should be self-evident. To winnow out from a vast population of consumers those individuals who are in fact interested in a particular product or service obviously takes considerable time, effort, and expense. Indeed, knowledge as to the identity of such individuals is a substantial factor in the value of a retail company's goodwill.

But commercial customer lists have also been protected as trade secrets where the identity of the commercial customers could not be easily compiled from public sources. For example, in one case former employees stole customer lists from a firm engaged in the esoteric occupation of selling sewage treatment plant operating manuals. The Minnesota Supreme Court ruled that the fact that the proposed sewage treatment facilities were identified in computer printouts prepared by state and federal environmental agencies did not make the identities of potential customers readily accessible. The reason: it would have been necessary to contact the city clerk about each municipality's project to determine the identity of the consulting engineer—a laborious and time-consuming undertaking. Therefore, the identity of prospective customers on the firm's lists was deemed protectable information.

Often the alleged reconstructability of commercial customer lists is more illusion than reality. In one case the defendant tried to show that a company's franchised distributors of business and accounting supplies could be compiled from telephone directories. The defendant was able to identify only 455 of 957 franchisees in this manner, and a quarter of those were wrong! This case illustrates how theoretical generalizations about the ready availability of information can be swept away by commerical realities.

Moreover, the fact that the identities of potential customers may be easily determined from industry directories and the like is of little more relevance in the commercial context than is the fact that customers of retail products and services are people and therefore can be found in a telephone directory. As every businessman knows, it is of far more interest to know who *is* buying than to know who *might*. As one California court noted in finding a list of customers for a certain type of advertising to be a trade secret: "It was the list of persons who *did* purchase plaintiffs' service that constituted confidential information. . . . [P]laintiff expended considerable time, labor and money in building up a list of subscribers who accepted and subscribed to their unique advertising medium; this group of merchants would be more likely to purchase such a service since they had already been 'sold' on its name as a method of advertising."

Indeed, some decisions indicate a predilection for protecting a customer list even where the universe of potential customers from which it was whittled down was relatively limited. In another California case, for example, the identities of stores and markets constituting the market for delicatessen products were ruled confidential, even though the identities of potential buyers, such as stores, meat markets, and delicatessens, could be obtained from the Yellow Pages and would obviously not be extensive. However, some courts have reached the opposite conclusion. Under similar circumstances other courts have held otherwise. In still another California case it was ruled that screening a list of hundreds of prospective steel purchasers—whose identities were well known from industry directories—to determine which were interested in buying a particular type of steel did not make the list of customers for that steel a trade secret. The court held that anyone could have obtained a similar list in the same manner the plaintiff had—by personal visits, letters, and advertising.

Let us now turn our attention from customer lists per se to the customer information and data often contained in such lists. The rationale for protecting confidential customer information has generally been the same as for the protection of customer lists themselves. First, it is thought to be inequitable to permit a competitor to benefit from another company's labors, not having had to expend the same time, effort, and resources to develop the information itself. Second, there is a perceived unfairness in permitting a former employee to abscond with customer data he then is able to use to deprive his former company of its customer base.

How a given case will be resolved usually depends on an individual judge's assessment of how much time, effort, and money has been dedicated to the compilation of the customer information. If the information is not readily accessible and the investment in the development of the customer information is substantial, a court would be more likely to regard its possession and use by a competitor to be fundamentally unfair. But if the customer data is freely available, the acquisition of customer information is more likely to be regarded as a component of an employee's general employment experience, which may be used in the service of a competitor.

All sorts of information have been asserted to constitute confidential customer information. We will consider each in turn.

Contact Personnel. Customer lists will frequently include the name of the person responsible for purchasing decisions. Some courts have held the identity of contact personnel to be confidential; others have not. Those courts finding in favor of the confidentiality of such information have stressed how time-consuming and costly it would be to ferret out the data independently. Those courts refusing to prevent former employees from utilizing customer lists containing this kind of information emphasize that anyone could have obtained it had he applied himself.

Although it is difficult to draw a differentiating principle from the cases, it does seem that the more numerous and geographically distributed the customers, the more likely that the identity of contact personnel will be treated as confidential. For example, the identities of purchasing authorities for polling machines sold to counties throughout the country were ruled to be confidential information. And the names of contact personnel for entities purchasing sanitary maintenance supplies were held confidential and protectable where the company sold to thousands of customers. On the other hand, in an early software case, the identities of contract administrators authorized to enter into custom software contracts were regarded as information readily available to anyone wishing to obtain it.

Customer Price and Discount Information.   We are concerned here with information about the price charged to individual customers outside the context of competitive bidding, which is treated elsewhere (see pp. 33–35). Although there are a few cases holding that customer pricing information can be protected from unauthorized use, courts have generally been unsympathetic to the proposition that prices charged to individual customers are in any sense confidential. The same has been true of such related charges as interest and finance charges. The reason for this is not hard to discern—customers frequently deal with more than one vendor, and they are more than happy to disclose the prices charged by a competitor in order to strike a better deal.

Unless a firm's customers or clients deal with that firm exclusively and customers are not making their purchase decisions based on ongoing comparisons of price and quality, it cannot really be said that customer information is anything but freely available. While companies may not like having their price quotes shopped around to their competitors, they cannot reasonably expect otherwise.

Credit Information.   Although credit data and information about a customer's financial status is by no means proprietary to the customer's suppliers, it is not, unlike price information, the sort of thing freely bandied about. One might therefore anticipate that claims that such information is confidential would fare better in the courts. This is in fact the case. Although several cases do assert that such information would either be generally known in the trade or could be easily discovered by investigation or by asking prospective customers, a respectable number of decisions have held that financial and credit information contained in a customer list should be considered confidential to the company that compiled it because of the time and expense involved. Once again, there is a relationship between the number of customers being served and the likelihood that customer credit and financial data will be treated as confidential.

Contract Expiration Dates. In any industry that sells a service for a specified period of time, such as a policy of insurance or an investment contract, the best time for a competitor to solicit the customer is at or near the contract expiration date. A number of cases have recognized the advantage that would thus accrue to an ex-employee in possession of his former employer's customer files. One court with an understanding of the marketplace wrote that the possession of renewal and expiration dates by an insurance agent opened his former employer to competitive attack at the most dangerous point—the date upon which the policies were to expire.

But the cases are not uniform. Occasionally a judge will invoke the familiar doctrine that expiration and renewal dates, like cost and coverage information, could readily be obtained from the consumer. However, this begs the real question, which is whether knowing *when* to call would confer upon an insurance company's or agency's former employee an unfair advantage he would not have had but for prior possession of his former employer's policyholder list. If it proved to be empirically true that soliciting policyholders at or near the date of expiration of their existing policies was more effective than calling at random times to ask them when their policies expired, then an agent's possession and use of a list containing expiration dates would manifestly deprive his former employer of a competitive advantage.

Customer Needs and Preferences. The category of customer information most often claimed to be confidential is a compilation of the needs, requirements, purchases, and preferences of customers. A number of courts have rebuffed efforts to have such information treated as confidential. However, the rationales advanced constitute gross oversimplifications of complex commercial realities.

Consider, for example, a case in which the former employee of a metal products distributor decamped, taking with him a book containing, among other things, the type and amounts of products purchased. The court denied trade secret status for such information on the ground that it would be available from other sources. But almost anything *could* be discovered, given world enough and time; the relevant inquiry should have been whether possession of the information would have materially assisted a competitor in securing the company's business. A breakdown of customer purchases by product will often be of invaluable assistance in obtaining or keeping a customer; indeed, one court was moved to assert that such information is "often more valuable to an entrepreneur than the physical plant."

What kinds of customer information are readily available should not be decided in a vacuum. It certainly may be the case in a given industry that customers consider the goods or services as commodities, so that the purchasing decision will be predicated exclusively on price and quality, and new suppliers with a lower price or a better product are welcomed. In such circumstances, customer information will be freely obtainable, and should not be considered confidential to anyone. But in the sale of speciality products or services, where the purchaser does not have the ability to independently evaluate competing products or relies on the reputation of, or personal relationship with, the supplier, there may be little inclination on the part of customers to disclose their purchasing decisions, requirements, or preferences to anyone but their trusted supplier.

There are other economic variables besides industry purchasing practices which must be evaluated as well. For example, in any industry facing a market composed of a significant number of customers who each purchase from one or only a few suppliers, the nature or volume of individual products each customer buys is certainly valuable information that is not going to be common industry knowledge, simply because of the structure of the industry. And regardless of the number of buyers, there will be times when a customer might deem it inadvisable to disclose its prior purchasing behavior or its future purchasing needs to suppliers bidding for its business. For example, if a supplier knew that a particular company required large numbers of one product, it could selectively discount from its published prices, whereas in the absence of such knowledge, an across-the-board discount might otherwise be forthcoming.

Thus, whether customer data is freely available in the industry is a question of fact to be determined from the evidence—not a matter to be blithely assumed. Not only the structure and practices of the industry, but also whether customer information was copied by the defendant and the motive for doing so, the percentage of the defendant's customers which were obtained from the plaintiff, and a host of other factors all enter the assessment of whether customer information is or is not readily available elsewhere.

Moreover, even if it were generally true that customers freely divulged the nature and volume of their purchases, this does not mean that a customer list disclosing such information would be of little competitive significance. In the world of commerce, time and expense are real, not theoretical, constraints. Just as knowing *when* to call could mean the difference between success and failure (as in the insurance context), knowing *which* customers to call on first—i.e., on which prospects to expend limited marketing and sales resources—could spell the difference between establishing a market position and becoming a market casualty. Particularly for the entrepreneur, who has limited resources almost by definition, knowing which customers buy which products in what volume, and which customers like which features in which products, would be an enormous advantage; indeed, this is what establishing a market niche is all about.

Finally, as with other categories of customer data, if the market is broad enough that obtaining customer data would be time-consuming and expensive, there is a certain element of unfairness in permitting a former employee to walk off with that kind of detailed information for the purpose of securing customers from his former employer.

For all these reasons, it is hard to support the general proposition that the identity of high-volume or single-source customers, or the particular purchasing patterns of individual customers, should not be treated as confidential information. And a number of courts have acknowledged that such customer data is confidential and protectable against unauthorized use.

Beside the contention that it is readily available, a couple of other rationales have been advanced for not treating customer data as confidential. One argument put forward is that data concerning customer needs and requirements should not be treated as confidential because they change. But this is not a rationale for *refusing* legal protection, only for limiting it as to time. The same argument could be made about other types of trade secrets; software is revised over time, industrial processes are altered, equipment is modified. This does not prevent such trade secrets from being protected for at least *some* time; the same should be true of confidential customer data.

A more serious concern has also been raised in several customer information cases. In the course of their employment, sales personnel become acquainted with the needs, requirements, and preferences of the customers they serve. It is, indeed, their stock in trade. Treating such information as confidential to the employer imposes a significant restraint on the employment mobility of sales personnel, and some courts have refused to treat such information as confidential on that ground. This particular problem is one facet of a larger issue—the differentiation of employee experience from an employer's proprietary information—which is treated extensively in Chapter 4. Suffice it to say here that the concern is a legitimate one, and care must be taken not to prohibit sales employees from utilizing their general sales knowledge and experience in competitive employment.

Competitive Bids and Bidding Practices

When a manager joins a firm that procures its work by competitive bid, he will invariably learn something about the firm's bidding practices. And if he becomes involved in the bidding process, he will not only learn the formulas by which bids are arrived at and the factors affecting each item in the calculation of costs, but he will also know how much has been bid on each job, what jobs will be coming available, and what jobs his employer has an interest in bidding on.

Is bidding information of this type a trade secret or confidential business information? Can employees be restrained from working for a competitor because they have become privy to such information? Or consider a tougher issue. Suppose an employee were to learn the details of a bid or proposal in the ordinary course of his employment and later joined a competing firm. Can the employee exercise his memory and utilize the information residing there to help his new employer prepare a competing bid?

The answers to these questions are not very definitive—it depends on which jurisdiction you are in and which judge you get. For example, one court ruled that information regarding proposals to prospective buyers of plywood veneer dryers was not confidential. The court was even moved to declare that the mere fact that the former employee of a manufacturer of the dryers knew what his former employer's bid to a certain prospect would be, and then submitted a competing bid $540 under his former employer's $168,000 bid, did not necessarily mean that the employee had used the information at his disposal! On the other hand, in a federal court decision the employee of a manufacturer of ozone production equipment had worked on a million-dollar installation proposal and then, after joining a competitor, had commenced work on a competing bid to the same municipality. The employee was aware of many of the details of his former employer's proposal but probably did not know the amount of the proposal itself. Not only was the employee enjoined from using such information, but he was enjoined from employment with the competitor *altogether* for a period of one year!

Thus, here, as with almost every other issue in this area of the law, there is a difference of opinion as to what represents fair use of information. Some people (and judges are people like everybody else, with their own personal notions of equity and fair play) think that using knowledge of a former employer's competitive bid is dirty pool, while others are more tolerant.

Finally, let us consider the most general case where knowledge of a specific bid or proposal is not an issue. Should an employee or his new employer incur liability for merely utilizing the employee's knowledge of his former employer's bidding practices or formulas?

The answer is unequivocal—unequivocally yes and unequivocally no, depending on the jurisdiction. Several courts have adopted the flat rule that bidding procedures or systems are not confidential or secret, not only because they are not kept secret by the company using them, but also because it can rarely be shown that they represent an advance in the state of the art or even an improvement over existing industry practice. A sensitive analysis of the issue by one federal judge convincingly makes the case against treating such information as legally protectable. The case involved a contention by a purchaser of petroleum coke for resale that the knowledge of its former employee (who was then working for a competing firm) as to its markup and overhead factors enabled the employee to predict what its bid was going to be and to respond accordingly. But the court observed that no matter how specific a bidding formula might be, in actual practice "[the mark-up and overhead factors] were fluid goals dependent on many variables of business oscillations which perforce do not become embedded into concrete restricted business confidences for all time." No company bids in a vacuum, and no matter what its general practice or its bidding formula might be, it must, from day to day, take into account general economic conditions, industry market conditions, the cost of money, its operating efficiency and capacity, and the price at which it can buy supplies. A New York judge put it succinctly: "The factors to be considered in making estimates are fundamental—inside costs, outside costs, overhead, and profit. The amount of money making up each factor necessarily fluctuates with the market. There is nothing secret in the decision of how much markup percentage is necessary for a good profit. Good estimating in this industry has the same common denominators as in others—experience and intelligence."

Nonetheless, such logic has not prevented some courts from entering injunctions against employees for the use of such information. When the vice president of a manufacturer of systems for ash and waste product disposal joined a competitor as president, his former company sued. The court found that the plaintiff's pricing formulas were confidential because the competitor's ability to bid was significantly enhanced by its ability to calculate plaintiff's costs on account of the pricing formulas known by its new president. But such a ruling fails to take into account all the manifold other factors affecting the submission of a bid far more than a set of formulas, and ignores the influence of other competitors in the bidding process. For example, if a company with 10 competitors knew the pricing formula of one of them, as a practical matter how much benefit would that really confer? Here, as elsewhere, holding business information to be confidential can have a significant adverse effect on employee mobility, and circumspection is in order.

Financial Information

Closely related to claims of confidentiality for bidding information is the assertion that financial data, in its manifold forms, is a trade secret. Profit and loss statements, price and cost data, capital spending plans, and budget allocations have all made their debut in trade secret litigation as purported company secrets.

As with other categories of information, the removal of financial data from the premises of an employer in some physical form usually results in legal liability. For example, in one instance a company maintained only one set of books containing raw material costs and commissions for its entire array of products, and only one person had unlimited access to the books. Such a compilation of data was held to be a trade secret because of the magnitude of the undertaking necessary to assemble it. There are a number of good policy arguments for such a ruling. First, a defecting employee could do much more damage removing cost books than having to rely on his own recollection of their contents. The frailty of human memory makes the loss of data collected through memorization a far less threatening event to a company than the misappropriation of its books and records. Second, an employee's removal of his employer's books and records containing financial data is often taken, not implausibly, as evidence of his intention to take advantage of the employer's trust in order to betray it—i.e., a classic breach of trust case. But such an inference cannot be drawn where the employee simply learned the details of a company's finances during the course of his employment and later changed employers.

But when it has not been misappropriated in tangible form, financial information obtained in the normal course of employment has not been regarded as trade secret subject matter. Thus, its possession by employees does not restrict their employment mobility or prevent them from accepting employment with a competitor. The most frequently advanced reason has been that much financial information, such as company profitability or costs of production, is common knowledge among managers and employees and is one of the components of that amorphous and ill-defined body of knowledge referred to as employee skill and experience. Claims of legal protection for financial information have also failed because the information was not in fact secret and was readily ascertainable from publicly available sources. A third rationale is that such financial information as price and cost data is a rapidly wasting asset, and quickly becomes outdated.

However, a few decisions have found strategically important financial information to be legally protectable against use by an employee. One court, for example, actually conferred trade secret status on such information as capital spending plans and budget priorities. Since so many employees within an organization are privy to financial information of one sort or another, care must be taken to circumscribe legal protection to information which is truly of competitive significance, lest employee mobility be unduly compromised and growing companies deprived of the services of qualified persons.

Advertising, Promotion, and Marketing Information

A survey reported in a *Harvard Business Review* article two decades ago revealed that there was more demand among business executives for competitive intelligence on pricing, promotion, and new product marketing than on technical matters. This survey serves to highlight the importance of marketing intelligence.

The courts' treatment of marketing information has, on the whole, been more consistent than for other categories of business information. Demands by companies for legal protection against former employees' use of knowledge of market demand for a product or service, of company marketing strategies and sales and marketing techniques, and of company advertising methods have repeatedly fallen on deaf ears. Judges have tended to regard this information as a facet of an employee's own skill, knowledge, and experience which he may use to his own betterment without restriction. Then, too, information regarding sales and advertising methods is almost antithetical to the notion of secrecy; the very purpose of marketing, advertising, and sales is *public promotion*, and the methods by which promotion is performed is necessarily disclosed along with the message being communicated.

There is, however, one category of marketing information that is *not* commonly reflective of an employee's general sales and marketing experience but is, like applied research, specific and directed: market research. Companies often pay small fortunes to determine what products to develop, how their products should be improved, how to make their products more acceptable to their customers, and how to market them most effectively. There is no reason such information should not be as secure from appropriation by an ex-employee as the products of technological research and development, and the courts concur. For example, when a company had conducted a market study and its market research had indicated that its magnetic visual display devices should be marketed only by mail order, only to certain types of businesses, and only to specific functional titles, and where the company had determined the sales return for the products advertised in its catalogues, this information was appropriately found to be a trade secret. Similarly, a market study disclosing a telephone company's projections as to the rate of replacement of old equipment and the corresponding schedule of new product introductions was held to be a category of information which could be a protectable trade secret. Information of this character is so specific and limited in scope as to advance only marginally an employee's general knowledge and skill, while use by an ex-employee would constitute a material deprivation of the benefits of a company's market research expenditures.

Marketing plans are another category of information which has enjoyed some degree of protection. Many corporations from time to time develop a comprehensive marketing plan for a specific product or service based on the accumulated experience of their marketing personnel. They assemble information from publicly available sources and apply well-known marketing techniques in a systematic and integrated way, resulting in higher sales or the opening of a new market. Such a marketing plan would certainly be for the most part merely an embodiment of general marketing expertise and public information. But it would at the same time constitute an aggregate of information in a specific form that did not exist before the market plan's creation.

Even though such marketing plans usually contain no element of "invention," in the sense of creating knowledge that did not exist before, the courts have tended to protect them against use by others without authorization. Market plans for the promotion and sale of prepaid funeral services, for the selling of insurance to federal employees, and for the marketing of seminars to quit smoking have all been held trade secrets. One rationale has been that even though each facet of the plan might have constituted common and well-known information, the marketing plan as a whole constituted a novel combination of such elements; for example, one decision specifically held that a marketing plan could be a trade secret unless it was publicly known in its specific form. This is another application of the principles relating to the issue of novelty discussed in Chapter 5.

Protecting marketing plans as trade secrets seems paradoxical, since they are necessarily disclosed by their execution. Consistent with this thinking, some years ago the Welcome Wagon method of marketing the products of sponsoring merchants was found not to be a trade secret because the method had obviously been disclosed to many people. But this argument has been advanced to little avail in more recent decisions.

Operations Information

It is hard to conceive of any more general and nonspecific business information than knowledge of a company's operations. Almost every employee has *some* understanding of a company's organization and procedures. No matter where an employee went to work within an industry, he would usually pick up the same sorts of knowledge (although the specific details might differ from company to company), and therefore such generic information could hardly be considered secret or confidential. In addition, any company would be hard pressed to show that the manner in which it conducted its business was maintained as a secret of the company.

For these reasons, a number of cases in a host of contexts have flatly ruled that knowledge of a company's business operations is neither secret nor confidential, but represents information that would generally be acquired by any employee working in the industry. Methods of operation of such entities as restaurants and transmission repair shops have been ruled not protectable against unauthorized use by others.

But there is also weighty authority to the contrary. For example, a company that evaluated the honesty and worthiness of charities on behalf of subscribers pursuaded a judge to find its methods of investigating new charities and interpreting the results to be trade secrets and to enjoin a former employee from using them in a competitive service. The novelty of the service might have provided a rationale for the result in that case, but methods of business operation have also been found to be confidential where no such rationale was available. In a California action, for example, an investment plan utilizing real estate secured loans was found to be confidential information which could not be used by a former employee even though the same information was distributed nationally by a mortgage company operation to its franchisees.

Indeed, knowledge of a company's business operations has even contributed in some cases to the issuance of an injunction against employment. In Pennsylvania, a vice president of an industrial gas supplier was enjoined from performing the same activities for a competitor because, among other things, he was familiar with his former company's research and development projects and the emphasis it placed on each; its novel methods of business operations in foreign countries; and its new methods of product delivery. The court reasoned that the identification of opportunities in the field as well as the extremely complex technological problems that had to be solved and commercial plans that had to be made to exploit these opportunities was enormously time-consuming and expensive, and that a competitor could appropriate the benefits of this information by hiring an employee who already possessed it. And in Ohio, an employee of a manufacturer of ozone and ozone apparatus in possession of business operating information was prohibited from working for a competitor *at all* for a period of time.

Admittedly, these cases involved key employees knowledgeable about many facets of their employer's business, not just operations matters; but the operations information was nonetheless a prominent feature of the decisions. Unfortunately, one finds in these cases no identification of the specific information deemed a trade secret, or why. Nor does one find in them a sensitive balancing of the interests in protection of business information on the one hand, and preservation of employee mobility on the other.

It must be kept in mind in considering the trade secret status of business operations information that virtually every senior management employee is privy to the methods, operations, and procedures of his company. To permit the possession of this type of information to become in effect a yoke around employees' necks is not only an unwarranted restriction on employee mobility but also seriously circumscribes the cross-fertilization of ideas, methods, and techniques that is so necessary to revive American industry at the present time.

The judicial debate over what business operations information is confidential extends to physical embodiments of that information. For example, the operations manual for the TGI Friday's restaurant chain wasn't found to be confidential, while a McDonald's operations manual was. Rather than indicating a preference for one cuisine over another, these two cases simply illustrate the disarray characterizing judicial treatment of business trade secrets.

The treatment of routine business forms has also been inconsistent. For example, when AAMCO Transmission sued a former franchisee the judge dismissed out of hand the claim that a form checklist the franchisee was using was a trade secret, concluding that the checklist represented "a formalization of procedures that would be followed by any service agency." But when several employees of a career counseling service formed a competing venture and used their former employer's written materials in violation of a covenant to the contrary in their employment agreements, they were held liable for breach of fiduciary duty *and* copyright infringement.

The Identities and Capacities of Suppliers

Perhaps the most frequently meritless trade secret claim asserted is that the identities of a company's suppliers are secret. There is an inherent contradiction in the contention that the identity of a supplier of goods or services, in the business of selling to the public, could be the trade secret of one of its customers.

A number of courts have agreed that the identity of a company's suppliers is a constituent part of an employee's knowledge and experience and is not the proprietary information of the employer. As with other forms of business information, the identity and capabilities of suppliers are types of information inevitably acquired by numerous employees within a company. If such information is regarded as a trade secret that employees can be prevented from using or disclosing, again the labor mobility of employees is seriously compromised. Equally important, if ex-employees can't inform their new employers of less expensive or higher quality suppliers, then higher productivity and quality will be thwarted.

Another reason cited for refusing to protect the identity of a company's suppliers has been the absence of any evidence that such information was in fact secret. A claim by a distributor of petroleum coke that its sources of coke were trade secrets was undone by the fact that petroleum industry publications identified not only the refineries that had coke for sale, but also the identity of the persons to contact.

Another common defect in the assertion that the identities of suppliers is a trade secret is that not many firms take any affirmative steps to keep this information confidential, and the failure to maintain adequate security precautions will often result in the loss of legal protection, for the information has thus become readily accessible to the world (see Chapter 6).

It must be acknowledged that there are a number of cases declaring in conclusory fashion that the identity of suppliers and the source of materials utilized in the manufacture of a product constitute a trade secret. Representative of these decisions is a California case involving a soldering tool manufacturer. A former officer and employee commenced competition with the company and was charged with misappropriating the company's trade secrets, including (among many other things) its sources of material. The court, upon a finding that substantial funds had been expended in the development of the information in the former employee's possession and that the company had taken reasonable precautions to protect the information from indiscriminate disclosure, prohibited the use of the company's trade secrets. But it is a highly dubious proposition that the company had expended much time or money at all in finding suppliers. There was certainly no evidence adduced in the opinion to indicate that that was a fact. Nor did the court determine whether the material suppliers were known in the industry or at least whether their identities were readily ascertainable from public sources. Finally, the court never considered whether the identity of a company's suppliers is not more properly characterized as part and parcel of an employee's general knowledge and skill, rather than the employer's proprietary information.

This decision indicates the mischief that can be done by conclusory rulings. When a company sues its ex-employee and cites a laundry list of trade secrets allegedly taken, it is incumbent on the court, laborious as the task might be, to carefully analyze each individual claim. What might seem to be a monstrous misappropriation in the aggregate can often be shown to be illusory when each category of information is considered separately on its own merit.

But this is not to say that supplier information should never be considered a legitimate trade secret. Removing documents containing such information is considerably different from learning about a company's suppliers in the course of employment. For example, when the president of a cleaning supply company left for a competing concern, he removed, among other things, closely guarded supplier books containing the identity of each supplier of chemical components, the price, shipping point, and salesman's name. The court reasonably deemed the books trade secrets, even though they were compiled from publicly available sources, because of the very considerable investment of time that the books represented.

But even the taking of supplier information in physical form has been a close question, and other courts have not been so liberal. For example, when an employee opened a branch office of a metal goods distributor and then took over the business himself, keeping his former employer's analysis of suppliers, the analysis was not accorded trade secret status.

There are a few cases legitimately holding the mere identities of suppliers to be trade secrets. For example, one company in the Southeast developed a water treatment purification system for air conditioner and boiler water that was superior to all other systems on the market, and none of its competitors could figure out how to duplicate the system's performance. The unusual aspect of the system was that it was put together entirely from components sold publicly, and the only way the company could keep its system secret was to obliterate the label and markings on each component. Here was a situation where mere identification of the suppliers would have disclosed the components of the system, resulting in the loss of the existing competitive advantage; so the identity of the component suppliers was properly regarded as a trade secret.

Another bemusing example is presented in an older California case where someone discovered (undoubtedly through painstaking research) that a particular type of cactus grew spines which could be used as phonograph needles. Only one species of cactus, which grew only in a particular area of Arizona produced suitable needles, and this information was protected from misappropriation by an unfaithful employee. Once again, this case presented something often claimed but rarely proved—a true secret source of supply.

Personnel Information

Personnel files contain a variety of more or less sensitive information. The employee's compensation level is certainly generally recognized to be a private matter, as are performance evaluations. The personnel file may also contain sensitive psychological evaluations or personality assessments.

Personnel information needs to be kept confidential for reasons extending beyond the need to preserve individual privacy. Besides capital, building, and equipment, a company needs good people—lots of them. And few managers who have been in business for long fail to appreciate that the single most important determinant of a venture's success or failure is the quality of its employees. Companies will therefore always be interested in recruiting qualified and capable employees; and what better opportunity to find experienced employees with proven track records than from competitors' ranks? But how to *identify* and successfully recruit such employees—*that* is the problem facing competitors lusting after a company's staff. This is why maintaining the confidentiality of personnel information is of such critical importance from a purely strategic perspective. Disclosure of personnel data could lead directly to the loss of a company's best employees and managers—the very lifeblood of the organization. Most companies don't steal personnel information outright; instead, a common tactic is to co-opt a key employee, pursuade him to leave his employment, and then elicit from him sensitive personnel information about his colleagues and subordinates.

The courts, however, have taken a dim view of this practice. They have held liable both the competitor eliciting the information and the employee disclosing it. One of the leading cases of this genre is a California decision, *Bancroft-Whitney Co. v. Glen,* where the president of Bancroft-Whitney was successfully recruited by Matthew Bender, a competing publishing company. In addition to other treacherous acts (such as gutting Bancroft-Whitney's organization by recruiting many of its employees while still on the Bancroft-Whitney payroll), the president also disclosed to Matthew Bender the identities of Bancroft-Whitney's best employees and their salaries, so that Matthew Bender would know who to recruit and how much to offer. The effectiveness of recruitment where such information is available was demonstrated by the fact that so many employees were induced to leave their jobs that it crippled Bancroft-Whitney's ability to compete. In unequivocal terms the California Supreme Court condemned this conduct, because such information was clearly confidential, and the officer was therefore violating a trust by revealing it to a competitor. And Matthew Bender was judged liable as well because it was found to have been aware of or to have ratified the officer's breach of fiduciary duty and to have received the benefits of that breach.

Another celebrated case, *Motorola, Inc.* v. *Fairchild Instrument and Camera Corporation,* is also instructive. In 1968, eight executives of Motorola resigned and joined a competitor, Of a whole laundry list of alleged violations of law, the only act the court deemed a breach of fiduciary duty was one of the Motorola officer's disclosure of the salaries that several other Motorola employees could command for their services.

Clearly, personnel data is one form of confidential business information that will be protected by the courts and may not be disclosed or extracted without risking legal liability.

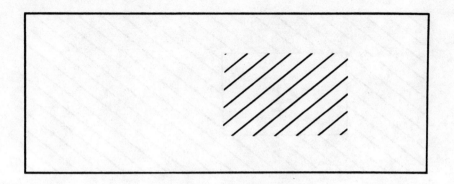

PART TWO

Social and
Economic
Policy
Implications

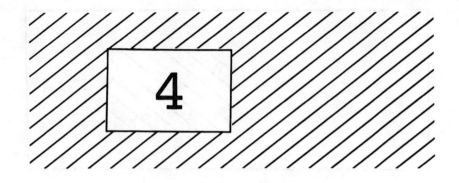

Employee Treachery or Employee Servitude?
Distinguishing between
Trade Secrets and
Employment Experience

Trade secret cases in general, and trade secret cases between employer and employee in particular, are not like typical commercial lawsuits, where the legal rights of the parties are adjudicated in an atmosphere of disinterested detachment. Instead, they are morality plays with a twist: Instead of Good and Evil being clearly identified, the judge and jury are left to sort out which party represents which. Before the case can be adjudicated, the conflicts between fundamental social and moral values presented in trade secret disputes must be resolved. In this regard, trade secret cases are more like politics than like common commercial disputes.

The Competing Policies

First and foremost among the conflicts between competing values trade secret disputes present is the tension between basic notions of property on the one hand and the interest in personal freedom and autonomy on the other. A company that spends large sums of money developing information giving it a competitive advantage rather naturally tends to regard that information as its own (i.e., as a form of "property") and regards its unauthorized use by others (including former employees) as a form of theft. An employee, on the other hand, who comes to the same information in the ordinary course of his employment responsibilities, and who perhaps improves on and enhances the nature or quality of the information, regards the content of his own thoughts as *his* own. He tends to regard restrictions on its use as compromising his ability to earn a living, thereby tying him to his existing employer in a sort of quasi-industrial bondage. He would also tend to regard such controls as an infringement of his personal freedom and autonomy.

Judges often become quite exercised over the clash of these opposing values. For example, one court, in finding for the employee, declared that trade secret protection "is not a sword to be used by employers to retain employees by the threat of rendering them substantially unemployable in the field of their experience should they desire to resign." This is prose uncharacteristic of a judicial opinion. In a similar style, the California Supreme Court has written that "public policy and natural justice require that equity should. . .be solicitous for the right inherent in all people . . .to follow any of the common occupations of life. . . . " These passages illustrate that when basic sociopolitical principles are at stake, disinterested discourse gives way to passionate engagement—even among judges.

The same property-autonomy conflict in the personal sphere has its counterpart in the public policy arena. A decision of the Pennsylvania Supreme Court cogently sets forth the public policy arguments in favor of restricting former employees' use of proprietary information:

> Society as a whole greatly benefits from technological improvements. Without some means of postemployment protection to assure that valuable developments or improvements are exclusively those of the employer, the businessman could not afford to subsidize research or improve current methods. In addition, it must be recognized that modern economic growth and development has pushed the business venture beyond the size of the one-man firm, forcing the businessman to a much greater degree to entrust confidential business information relating to technological development to appropriate employees. While recognizing the utility in the dispersion of responsibilities in larger firms, the optimum

amount of "entrusting" will not occur unless the risk of loss to the businessman through a breach of trust can be held to a minimum.

There are clearly compelling reasons to afford protection to company proprietary information. But the protection of information from use by employees is a two-edged sword. The greater the protection afforded, the lesser may be the rate of technological innovation and its concomitant social and economic benefits. Several recent studies have found that there is much more technological innovation and new job formation from small firms than from the large corporate monoliths. Strict restraints on the use of information obtained in prior employment tends to inhibit entrepreneurial venture formation by employees wishing to start companies or join growing firms to exploit their own expertise and ideas. Restrictions on the use of information in the possession of an employee also prevents, to borrow a phrase from property law, the highest and best use of the employee's capabilities, as well as restricting the free flow of ideas and reducing competition.

It is because the social policy considerations are often in near equipoise that trade secret disputes between employer and employee are so difficult to resolve. Compounding the problem is the circumstance that most cases are not simply claims for money damages. They also involve a request to invoke the coercive authority of the state—through the application of the court's injunctive powers—to stop the use or disclosure of company proprietary information.

Obviously, there has to be some limitation on the restrictions companies can place on the use of information their employees obtain during the scope of their employment. Otherwise, a company could assert that none of the knowledge and experience each employee gained during his tenure could be used in the service of another, and industrial servitude would become a stark reality. Accordingly, there is little dispute among courts with the basic proposition that an employee's opportunity to use the general knowledge, skill, and experience he has obtained during the course of his employment may not be restricted.

But differentiating between general employee knowledge and skill on the one hand and company proprietary information on the other can be almost an occult science. For one thing, no one is going to know, at the margin, what is common knowledge in the industry, even assuming one could define "common" satisfactorily. At any given time, no particular company in an industry is going to know about all the processes, techniques, or devices its competitors know and use. But performing an information "audit" of the industry to establish the state of the art is often next to impossible without an expensive investigation of the devices and processes used by a representative sample of one's competitors. And the exercise of the subpoena power against competitors, prospective customers, or suppliers, while conducting such an investigation could make a company an industry pariah. A less offensive way to establish the state of an industry's knowledge is to employ an expert witness familiar with industry practices, but an expert witness may have no better basis for making such an assessment than anyone else; besides, the opponent would just proffer its own expert in rebuttal.

Moreover, many trade secret disputes involve knowledge that cannot neatly be classified as "general employee knowledge" or "company proprietary information" even if industrial practice could be easily established. For example, learning the details of technologies well known in the industry clearly would fall within the rubric of "general employee knowledge and experience"; but what about an employee's refinements and modifications of those technologies?

Indeed, do developments which are clearly an advance over the industry state of the art become company proprietary information or part of the experience of the employee who performed the development? Such issues border on—or cross over into—the field of epistemology, and while they might make for good philosophical discussion, they make for bad law. The rationales offered by judges—when they offer any explanation at all—as to when information is proprietary to a company and when it is employee knowledge and experience simply make no sense.

Rather than try to construe the incantations of courts that have tried to define just what employee knowledge and experience really is, it would be more useful to draw certain empirical conclusions from the holdings of the cases discussing the issue.

Empirical Rules of Decision

Enhancements in Employee Skill

Most courts have concluded that enhancements in an employee's general skill and experience such as would normally be obtained by one similarly employed may freely be used by the employee without any restriction whatever. This is true notwithstanding the fact that the employee's gain in knowledge and experience may have been substantial or may have resulted from comprehensive training the employer provided at considerable expense.

For instance, in a recent Massachusetts case a company sued a former employee who had helped develop a management information system and then resigned to develop a similar system for a competitor, seeking to prevent him from using the knowledge he had acquired during the course of his former employment. The court, after rejecting the claim that the management information system was a trade secret, stated that the employee was entitled to use his enhanced experience in the service of a competitor, noting that "it is just such exposure and activities which are part of the experience that enters into the knowledge and skill which define a scientist or engineer."

But this attitude is not invariable. In one case involving the alleged theft of trade secrets relating to shoe manufacturing machinery, the court assessed the defendant employee's state of knowledge as of the time he had *commenced* his employment. This effectively deprived the employee of the argument that the information alleged to have been improperly taken represented no more than his own general knowledge and experience acquired during the course of employment.

Mere Refinements and Modifications in Well-Known Technologies

An employee's minor refinements to well-known technologies are frequently considered to be part of an employee's own knowledge and experience. For example, in one well-known case a chemist had been employed to analyze and duplicate competitors' products and then use them as a basis for developing new formulas. The chemist left to join a competitor, and his former employer brought suit to prevent him from disclosing or using the formulas he had developed. But the Pennsylvania Supreme Court concluded that because the formulas had been derived without experimentation or research and represented little more than reverse engineering with minor modifications, they should be considered the mere fruits of the chemist's own skill and knowledge, and his use of such information did not constitute a breach of confidence.

The Highly Skilled Employee

Another good empirical guideline in trade secret disputes is that companies who sue employees who were hired because they had substantial directly applicable prior experience usually lose. There are a number of reasons for this result.

First, the adverse consequences to the employee of granting trade secret protection to the employer are greatest in such circumstances. Any restraint on his ability to use the knowledge and experience he obtained in his last job will also circumscribe his ability to use *all* knowledge and experience acquired during prior employment as well, since the two are inextricably intertwined.

Second, where an employee has substantial prior experience, it becomes correspondingly more difficult for his employer to show that any given process, device, or the like was derived from the employer's proprietary information rather than from the employee's own extensive background. For example, an engineer who had designed a number of centrifugal pumps for a business he owned later sold his company and formed a competitive venture making similarly designed pumps. His former company sued. Even though the engineer had removed hundreds of blueprints when he left, the court nonetheless concluded that the new company's designs were derived from the engineer's own prior experience, rather than from the drawings that had been removed from the plaintiff's premises. Since he had originally designed the plaintiff's pumps, it was hard to argue that the similar pumps manufactured by his new company were anything but the product of the employee's own prior experience. Not until the employee has moved afield from his prior experience can his former employer plausibly claim that any contribution made by the employee was not the product of what the employee already knew.

Finally, when a company hires an employee with substantial prior experience, it is almost compelled to concede that enhancements in the employee's experience acquired at the company would not constitute proprietary information. Otherwise, it would have to admit that enhancements of experience in the service of *other* companies were *also* proprietary, and that by hiring the employee the company was trying to gain access to his previous employers' trade secrets and proprietary information. In one case the judge, in ruling against a semiconductor company that had hired several experienced employees to renovate its semiconductor manufacturing machinery, pointedly observed that it could be presumed from the fact that the company had hired experienced employees from a competitor that the company did not consider their knowledge and experience to constitute a trade secret.

As with everything else in trade secret law, there is authority to the contrary, however. Under circumstances similar to the aforementioned centrifugal pump case, an Illinois court came to precisely the opposite conclusion. The president of a hypodermic needle manufacturer, with years of experience in product and machine design, had diverted design drawings to another firm that he had formed. The court found, as in the pump case, that the officer *could* have reproduced the plans on account of his expertise in the industry. But the fact that he *did not,* but instead took the plans, rendered him liable.

It is troubling when two courts, on very similar facts, resolve the matter in diametrically opposite ways. But at least this case has a reasonable rationale: that the employee, by the exercise of his experience and skill, could have recreated the plans did not prevent the plans themselves from being trade secrets which he was not free to take. Other cases involving highly skilled employees are of more concern. In *Modern Controls Inc.* v. *Andreadakis* an employee possessing a Ph.D in physics helped develop a flat panel gas discharge display device (like a cathode ray tube, for use in computers) for Control Data. He was then hired away from Control Data by Modern Controls, and put to work commercializing *the same device.* But when he quit and went to work for Burroughs developing a similar device, Modern Controls sued him! Modern Controls sought to enforce a non-competition agreement preventing him from working for Burroughs on the ground that Andreadakis was in possession of its confidential business information. He argued, not surprisingly, that when he left Modern Controls he did not know anything he did not already know when he came to Modern Controls from Control Data. But the court held that since the device was transformed from an unmarketable to a marketable state during the period of his employment at Modern Controls, he *must* have learned *something* that was confidential.

To enjoin a highly trained employee from working in his area of expertise—especially when he was the one who developed the concept in the first place—on the mere conjecture that he must have learned something confidential during later development work is manifestly inappropriate. Once the basic design work was concluded, it is more probable—if one wishes to engage in conjecture—that what followed to commercialize the product represented merely the application of general employee experience and well-known engineering principles.

Public policy weighs heavily against restraining extremely experienced and knowledgeable employees from practicing their art. Courts should not permit the information they already possess to be transmuted, by legal incantation, into the trade secrets of their employers, so that employers can terrorize competitors for the effrontery of hiring away their former key employees.

Experimentation, Objectives, and General Know-How

Suppose an engineer, over the course of his employment, comes to appreciate the problems that must be solved to achieve a certain research objective, which research avenues might be fruitful, and which avenues of research had not proved fruitful to pursue. Is such nebulous information general employee knowledge and experience or proprietary research information? Most researchers would probably laugh at the very idea that information of such a nature could be considered a trade secret, and would be horrified to learn that the issue has been hotly litigated.

Employees have fared reasonably well in cases involving such inchoate information, although the results have certainly not been uniform. In a Massachusetts case, for example, a company's director of research had had occasion to reflect on certain product ideas concerning a particular type of gasket, in furtherance of which he conducted experimentation that proved unsuccessful. Later, he formed his own company and proceeded to successfully develop the products himself. His former employer sued, asserting that the information he gained as its research director was confidential and proprietary. But the court rejected the proposition that the identification of research objectives could be proprietary to an employer: "[T]hat [the defendant] had worked on these possibilities and goals for [his former company] or that they occurred to him while at [his former company] does not make them...any the less a part of his experience and development as a scientist which he was entitled to use. . . ." And in another case, a vending machine manufacturer complained that its former employees had successfully manufactured vending machines containing features it had been trying to develop. The court ruled that goals and objectives, as opposed to the means of achieving them, could not be treated as company trade secrets.

But an appreciation of problems and objectives has not invariably been excluded from the realm of trade secret protection. In Pennsylvania it was ruled that an appreciation of the technical problems associated with enhanced petroleum recovery systems and an understanding of what safety precautions were necessary constituted components of company trade secrets. The court prohibited an employee from using this information in subsequent employment even where such a working knowledge of technical problems was the product of work the employee had done himself.

Knowledge of the results of experimentation—whether organized or trial and error—has also been the focus of trade secret litigation. For example, when a research director for Minnesota Mining and Manufacturing who had supervised the development of a precision tape recorder founded his own company and began manufacturing the same device, Minnesota Mining and Manufacturing instituted a suit for trade secret misappropriation. The suit alleged (among other things) that the knowledge of what mistakes to avoid and how to proceed in the development of a precision tape recorder were trade secrets. The appellate court severely criticized the trial court's ruling that this type of knowledge could constitute a trade secret. The court observed that such a broad construction would be tantamount to prohibiting the research director from conducting any research and development in the same area at all, for it would have been patently impossible for him to exclude from his mind "what not to do" in any subsequent research activity. And other courts have denied trade secret protection to that intangible quality sometimes referred to as employee "know-how," consisting of the accumulated benefit of on-the-job experience and results of trial and error, leading to improved production or a better product.

But not all courts have been of such a mind. For instance, the Missouri Supreme Court ruled that experimentation not resulting in a commercially viable product was confidential company information, at least where the employee privy to the results of such research had signed a nondisclosure agreement promising not to disclose any information relating to the inventions, processes, or methods of the company's business. But if knowledge of unsuccessful experimentation can be transformed into proprietary company information by recitals in a nondisclosure agreement, there does not appear to be any reason why *all* knowledge and experience gained during the course of an employee's tenure could not be so transformed. This ruling also runs counter to the doctrine that courts will not honor a nondisclosure agreement's recitals about what constitutes confidential information, but will instead make their own independent assessment (see p. 111).

Applying Known Techniques

If an employee has learned how to apply generally known knowledge and techniques to achieve a not well known result, does such knowledge partake of the nature of general employee experience or is it proprietary company information? That is a central question in employee trade secret disputes because it is at this intersection between the two classes of information that irreconcilable differences of opinion occur.

In some cases the application of well-known techniques to achieve an innovative or superior result has been considered the by-product of an employee's own knowledge and experience. Therefore, information so acquired was deemed a mere extension of that knowledge and experience. For example, in one case the former president of a medical products company, who held a doctorate in immunology and microbiology, had during the course of his employment developed a number of immuno-fluorescent techniques and formulations used in diagnostic kits sold by the company. After losing a proxy fight, he was fired, and he thereupon organized a competing venture. His former company then sued him for misappropriation of trade secrets. In finding against the company, the Utah Supreme Court rationalized its decision by noting that each of the techniques the defendant used in developing the company's products he had learned in graduate school many years before, and he had merely applied what he knew already to accomplish what his former employer later claimed as its trade secrets. Similarly, a chemist who had been closely involved with the development of a commercial process for making cyclamates was sued when he formed a rival company. It was acknowledged by the court that the chemist had acquired from his employer "certain knowledge of particular engineering techniques which could be applied at a given point more advantageously than another technique," but the ability to know what techniques would work was deemed a component of the chemist's own skill and experience.

But other courts have regarded knowledge of the novel or superior product of the application of well-known techniques to be proprietary to a company. For example, the use of an annular air jet to remove industrial exhaust gases has been well known for some time; nonetheless, a New Jersey court ruled the incorporation of annular air induction into a tennis ball throwing machine to be a trade secret that could not be used by former directors of a tennis ball machine manufacturer. Similarly, when two former employees of Head Ski Company were sued for using Head's manufacturing trade secrets, the employees responded that Head's methods of construction couldn't be trade secrets because they were all widely known to and used by aircraft mechanics. But the court's response to this argument was brief and succinct: "This overlooks the fact that a knowledge of the particular process, method or material which is most appropriate to achieve the desired result may *itself* be a trade secret." The judge went so far as to say that even though many of the alleged trade secrets would have been disclosed by subjecting skis available on the open market to material testing, just knowing what tests to utilize was a trade secret learned by the former employees.

The Problem of the Employee-Developer

What seems to be at the heart of many of the cases discussed in the previous section was not so much what the nature of the information was, but what constituted fair *use* of information an employee learns during the course of employment. A few recent decisions have explicitly adopted a "comparative interest" analysis. Venturing tentatively into uncharted territory, these decisions have looked not to the character of the *information* acquired during the course of employment, but rather to the respective *interests* of employer and employee in such information.

Sole Development

Perhaps the landmark case of this genre is *Structural Dynamics Research Corporation* v. *Engineering Mechanics Research Corporation.* Here employees who had developed structural analysis software formed a competitor and developed a competing program. The judge ruled that the employees' use of technology which *they themselves had originally created* did not constitute a breach of confidence because under such circumstances "the employee may then have an interest in the subject matter at least equal to that of his employer." This case clearly proposed a new legal calculus to be used in employer-employee trade secret disputes when the employee has developed the trade secret at issue. Several other decisions have followed a similar analysis.

Resolving employer-employee disputes over the use of confidential information by assessing the relative interests and contributions of each makes eminent good sense. Trying to apply the "general knowledge and experience" standard can only lead to inconsistent resolution of cases, and injustice to at least some litigants, because the concept defies definition. Like beauty or obscenity, "general knowledge and experience" are basically in the eyes of the beholder. Indeed, what constitutes general knowledge and experience has as much to do with the knowledge and experience of the person assessing the matter as with the facts of any particular case.

Predicating the permissible scope of use of information on the relative interests of employer and employee in the development of that information also leads to intuitively equitable results. Consider, for example, a customer list trade secret case where an employee, such as a route salesman or driver, has not only serviced his route but substantially enlarged it by soliciting new customers and calling on old friends and acquaintances. In some jurisdictions, the identity of such customers is a trade secret belonging to the employer whether or not the employee contributed to their procurement. But the Minnesota Supreme Court held that in cases of this kind, the right of a route salesman to change employers and then solicit his old customers depended on the scope and extent of his contribution to the development of the customer list so that where an employee has himself built up patronage for his employer's product or service "he may share with the employer the right to solicit and enjoy the fruits of his labor after the termination of his employment." Other decisions have reached similar results; employees who had developed their own records of customers or industry contacts were permitted to use them simply because they themselves had prepared them.

There is another rationale for conferring on an employee the right to use information he developed in his prior employment—one which will take on added significance as the course of economic decentralization, now already gathering momentum, accelerates. A number of years ago an employee well known in the industry as an aircraft ejection seat system designer was fired. He formed his own company and submitted to an aircraft company a proposal to supply precisely the same device he had been designing in his previous employ. His former employer thereupon sued for trade secret theft. But because it was found to be the industry practice for mainframe manufacturers to deal with the principal investigator—not his company employer—on an experimental project, the court ruled that the corporate employer could not assume that it was invested with all rights to the knowledge and information developed during the project—

particularly since the company's efforts to obtain such exclusive rights from the employee by contract had previously been rebuffed. Because the employee dealt with customers on a quasi-independent basis, he retained the right to use information he developed in his prior employer's employ.

Joint Development

Where the employer and the employee have both devoted substantial resources and effort to a development effort, different considerations obtain. The most common example is the participation of a particular employee in a major research and development program. It would be extremely difficult in such circumstances to separate the employee's contribution from the contribution made by others in the company. And it would be even more difficult to try to enforce a court decree whereby the employee could use the information he had developed but not any of the knowledge he had gained by virtue of the efforts of others. In addition, companies just aren't going to make the sizable R&D expenditures necessary to keep American business competitive if any R&D employee could walk out the door with the fruits of that research.

From a theoretical point of view one could say, to use comparative-interest analysis, that where the employer has made substantial contributions to an R&D effort through the dedication of research personnel and the expenditure of large sums of money, the employer's economic interest resulting from its contribution exceeds the interest of any individual employee participating in it. Therefore, no employee should have any legally recognized right to use such knowledge for his own purposes. Alternatively, to use more traditional theories, it might be said that by virtue of the substantial expenditure of company resources in a research and development effort, every participating employee knows he is under a duty not to use or disclose the knowledge acquired through such an effort.

Whatever the rationale, whenever there has been a substantial contribution by the employer to the acquisition of knowledge or the creation of a new product or process, employees have usually not been accorded a right of equal use, even when their contribution exceeded that of any other person. For example, the founders of National Semiconductor Corporation, former employees of Sperry Rand, were held to have misappropriated Sperry Rand's trade secret semiconductor manufacturing processes—a process they themselves had substantially developed—

on account of Sperry Rand's considerable expenditure of resources in the development of the production process. And in an Iowa case the fact that the former president of a chemical company had developed his former company's formulas was held to not accord him a right of equal use, in view of the company's expenditure of time and money in the research that yielded those formulas. Indeed, in one case where an oil company geologist formulated a theory indicating the presence of oil in a particular geological formation, the court ruled this knowledge to be proprietary to the company and not to be used by the employee even though the theory was entirely developed by the employee and even though the oil company's only contribution was permitting the employee use of its confidential geological data. Any material contribution by a company to the development of commercially valuable information will usually vitiate any right the employee-developer might have to use that information for his own ends. But on occasion a court will tolerate an employee's use of a device or process he contributed to, even where the project represented a substantial investment for the company. In one decision, a chemist was permitted to use his knowledge of a cyclomate production process in the service of a rival even though the company had spent many years and substantial money in developing the process.

The Dilemma of the Confidentiality Agreement

Even those courts that recognize an employee's right to use proprietary information which he himself developed have nonetheless upheld confidentiality agreements signing away that right. In the *Structural Dynamics* case, the trial judge upheld a nondisclosure agreement signed by the employees who had developed the structural analysis program whereby the employees agreed not to use or disclose the confidential information of the company. Because the agreement did not, by its express terms, *exclude* from its operation confidential information the employees themselves had brought into being, and since the structural analysis program was deemed confidential, the employees could not utilize what they had learned while creating it. In other cases as well employees have been barred from utilizing information they themselves developed because they had signed employee nondisclosure agreements.

The application of nondisclosure agreements to entirely employee-developed information presents a serious public policy issue. In the abstract, there is nothing objectionable about an employee, in return for employment or some other benefit, waiving any common-law right he might have to use knowledge he himself developed. But nondisclosure agreements are not signed in the abstract; they are signed in the aggregate, by tens of thousands of employees. And in the aggregate, there is no semblance of arms-length negotiation, no reservation by the employee of rights in information developed by the employee, and usually no thought given by the employee to the consequences of signing a company confidentiality agreement. The use of such agreements is becoming more common every day, and signing them is, at many companies, a prerequisite of employment.

In an "information society," where the number of employees whose principal occupation is the development, refinement, and processing of information is increasing, the extent and scope of significant employee-created trade secret information will be commensurately great. And in this country most technological innovation and new job formation has been generated by small entrepreneurial firms. The enforcement of confidentiality agreements as to trade secrets created by an employee without any appreciable contribution by his employer would not merely impinge on the career opportunities of the employees concerned, but could also affect the rate of technological innovation in this country.

This is not to say that nondisclosure agreements should *not* apply to employee-developed information. The employer has strong arguments in support of a contrary position. For example, why should an employee be permitted to use information he was well paid to create, a company might ask. And wouldn't such a policy give employees an incentive to conceal their work from their employers? The jury is still out on these issues. But we need to recognize that employees' use of information they themselves have created presents a public policy question; it is not simply a private matter between the parties to a confidentiality agreement.

5

Trade Secret, Trade Practice, Trade Knowledge, Public Knowledge
Distinguishing the Figure in the Field

Next to distinguishing between an employee's knowledge and experience on the one hand and a company's proprietary information on the other, perhaps the most intransigent issue in trade secret law is the differentiation of information proprietary to a company from knowledge possessed by the trade or the public in general. Unlike patent law, which requires that a discovery represent a distinct advance in the state of the art that would not occur to one skilled in the trade, a trade secret need not meet such a high standard of innovation. But absent a strict test for defining trade secret subject matter, the line between public information and proprietary information is so blurred as to be virtually indistinct. At the margin, the question of whether a particular form of information falls on one side of the line or the other reduces itself almost to a matter of opinion.

Not only are the categories of information subject to trade secret protection almost limitless (as we discovered in Chapter 3), but the breadth of protection is not well appreciated. The public has little conception of how intrinsically simple information can be and still qualify as a protectable trade secret. A decision half a century ago vividly expresses this point:

> The mere fact that the means by which a discovery is made are obvious, that experimentation which leads from known factors to an ascertainable but presently unknown result may be simple, we think cannot destroy the value of the discovery to one who makes it. . . . Facts of great value may, like the lost purse upon the highway, lie long unnoticed upon the public commons.

A few illustrations will indicate how really mundane a trade secret can be. In one instance several enterprising entrepreneurs came up with the idea of pressing a facecloth into the shape of a small drum, which would expand to full size when immersed in water. Others, intrigued with the product, obtained the details of the procedure under the guise of seeking a license to market it, and then went into competition with the originators of the product. In the ensuing lawsuit, it was claimed that the product's originators *had* no trade secret to be misappropriated. But the court, while acknowledging that the idea may have seemed simple, pungently observed that interested persons such as the defendants had not in fact thought of the idea themselves. Similarly, in another decision it was ruled that the discovery that putting artificial sweetener tablets in a low-humidity room for a couple of days before packaging lengthened shelf life was a trade secret. All that it was necessary to show, the court said, was that the idea was original enough to distinguish it from mere common knowledge.

Modest improvements in well-known devices, processes, or machinery can also qualify as trade secrets. In one decision, an engineer in the employ of a cashmere producer adapted machinery used in the combing of raw cotton to the separation of cashmere from fleece. The design for this machinery was later misappropriated by a competitor, and in the ensuing lawsuit the competitor asserted by way of defense that the machinery did not in fact embody any trade secrets. The trial judge agreed, stating that to simply adapt well-known machinery to a different application did not rise to the level of a trade secret. But the appeals court reversed, holding that no more novelty than the simple adaptation at issue was necessary for there to be a protectable trade secret.

Closely related to whether mere adaptations of well known equipment or processes can be trade secrets is whether a *combination* of them can be a trade secret.

In a number of cases combinations of elements all of which were well known have been found to be trade secrets on account of the commercial superiority of the combination. No case better illustrates the point than *Water Services, Inc.* v. *Tesco Chemicals, Inc.*, where a system for the treatment of water circulating in boilers and air conditioners was claimed to be a trade secret. Every single one of the components of the system could be purchased on the open market by anyone knowing what parts to buy. But because identifying marks and features of the components had been obliterated, no one could determine the source of the components from an inspection of the system. Despite the fact that not a single part of the system could be characterized as secret and despite the fact that the water treatment system had been marketed for years, none of the manufacturer's competitors had been able to duplicate its capabilities. Because the whole was obviously greater than the sum of the parts, the system was held to constitute a trade secret despite the absence of any novelty of design or advance in the state of the art. Plainly speaking, the system was found to be a trade secret simply because it worked better than anyone else's.

But the issue is still open. Manufacturing processes is one of the arenas in which the debate as to whether combinations of commonly known elements can constitute a trade secret has reached conflicting conclusions. On one hand there is a Michigan decision that held a process for chrome-plating axle shafts not to be a trade secret *even though no one had been able to do it profitably before, and even though it had required development and experimentation before the process was perfected*, because the individual steps in the process were known in the industry. On the other hand, in a case involving semiconductor manufacturing processes the facts that the steps in the process may have been known in the literature and the individual equipment, materials, and procedures utilized may also already have been known in the semiconductor industry or elsewhere was deemed to be irrelevant since "there was no evidence at all that substantially the same pieces of equipment, materials and procedures had been used substantially in the same way and for substantially the same purpose by anyone."

One finds the same inconsistency with regard to other forms of information as well. In the software context, the Minnesota Supreme Court found graphics software in a CAD/CAM (computer-aided design and manufacturing) system not to be a trade secret because it represented no more than the adaptation of standard software elements and did not embody any novelty or innovation. Yet a Michigan federal judge ruled that structural analysis software was protectable confidential information even if all of its elements could be found in the engineering literature, declaring that a novelty and uniqueness requirement had been rejected by "an overwhelming majority of authorities."

Similarly, in the marketing context one court ruled a franchisor's merchandising program not to be a trade secret because it was not novel and represented no more than an efficient packaging of what was already well known. However, another court, rejecting a novelty requirement, found a marketing plan for the sale of insurance to federal employees to be a protectable trade secret even though all of the material used was derived from information and techniques in the public domain, because the integrated combination of materials and techniques conferred a competitive advantage.

It is apparent what is at the heart of these two diverging lines of cases. If a "novelty" or "uniqueness" standard of innovation is applied, the court rules there is no trade secret. But if simple commercial advantage is the standard for determining whether there is a trade secret, the plaintiff frequently wins its trade secret claims.

There is no practical reason for applying a novelty standard—a concept derived from patent law—for trade secret protection. It must be borne in mind that unlike the patent laws, which confer an absolute monopoly of 17 years' duration, trade secret law confers legal protection only against the acquisition of a trade secret by improper means or the disclosure of information in breach of a confidence. As is observed in the legal treatise, the Restatement of Torts: "[F]or this limited protection it is not appropriate to require. . .the kind of novelty and invention which is a requisite of patentability." A commercial superiority standard is quite sufficient to distinguish a trade secret from the commonly known, for that which is *truly* obvious would occur to those skilled in the trade, and there would be uniformity in the industry, not commercial superiority by one company.

Nothing more graphically illustrates this point than a case brought by Rohm & Haas to prevent a former employee's misappropriation of its process for making paint. The product resulting from the process was so competitively superior that a competitor launched a massive R&D effort to duplicate it, and after achieving success in the lab the competitor made a new product announcement to the trade. However, its efforts to commercialize the process failed, leaving it in desperate straits. Indeed, in order to fill orders, it went to the extreme of purchasing Rohm &

Haas paint and repackaging it. Obviously its motivation to develop a successful commercial process could not have been greater; yet it was not able to do so until it hired a former Rohm & Haas employee familiar with the Rohm & Haas paint production process.

Unable to point to any particular aspect of its process that was not well known in the industry, Rohm & Haas was compelled to argue that the process as a whole was obviously not known in the industry because it produced a commercially superior product whose features had not been matched by competitors despite their strong economic incentive and efforts to do so. But because Rohm & Haas could not specify how its process differed from either general employee knowledge and experience in the industry or techniques commonly used in the trade, the trial judge rejected Rohm & Haas' "commercial superiority" analysis, and denied trade secret protection. But the appellate court emphatically disagreed, and ordered the entry of a permanent injunction prohibiting the use of the Rohm & Haas process, reasoning that it was a protectable trade secret simply because it resulted in a competitively superior product.

When a company has developed a product or process which is better than the competition, there may be some legitimate rationale as to why competitors didn't duplicate it. But the reasons that come most readily to mind are that the competition didn't think of it, or that they couldn't do it.

It is one thing to show how an improvement can be derived from common industry practice after you already know how to do it; it is quite another to think of it yourself in the first place. As a judge acidly observed in one case: "only a person who knew the...process could make the selection of literature references which were offered in evidence" to show the process was not a secret. Whether an advance is sufficiently innovative to be protected as a trade secret should turn not on what some hypothetical person skilled in the trade *might* have derived from industry knowledge and practice had he thought about it, but rather on how the industry did *in fact* respond to a competitor's technological improvement. Certainly where a competitor has tried and failed to duplicate a competitively superior product or process, that is strong evidence that the improvement could not in fact be readily derived from industry practice or the available literature, and *post hoc* efforts to demonstrate the contrary should be unavailing.

There are other reasons why the assembly of known elements to attain a commercially superior but technologically uninnovative result should be recognized to constitute a trade secret. It makes no more sense to argue, for example, that a piece of machinery is not a trade secret because it is composed of commonly used components than it does to argue that a novel is not original because it is made up of commonly used words. It is the *relationship* of the constituent elements of any type of work—be it mechanical, electronic, or literary—that distinguishes it from the commonplace. The combining of known elements into a commercially superior product can be likened to the creation of a recipe from commonly available ingredients; the whole is very much more than the sum of the parts.

Finally, requiring novelty in trade secret cases leads to the intractable problem of determining what is novel and what isn't, which in turn requires an assessment of what one ordinarily skilled in the trade could have done. Such an inquiry leads to difficult epistemological speculations. For example, one court defined a trade secret as that which "is of a character which does not occur to persons in the trade with knowledge of the state of the art, or which cannot be evolved by those skilled in the art from the theoretical description of the process, or compilation or compendia of information or knowledge."

But how could a jury, a judge, or *anyone*, lacking an intimate technical knowledge of the subject matter, be expected to properly make such judgments? In assessing novelty in patent cases, one at least has the benefit of knowing that a significant improvement over the existing state of the art must be shown. But in trade secret cases, the judge or jury has to make judgments much closer to the line separating the innovative from the commonly known. In addition, what is commonly known may be apparent to the industry but isn't necessarily obvious to the judge or jury. How can we expect fine distinctions to be drawn where *neither* the alleged trade secret nor industry practice are well understood by judge or jury?

Like undiscovered "windows of opportunity" in the marketing sphere, there often exists undiscovered opportunities for minor technological improvements or new combinations of old technologies that result in a better product or a more efficient or inexpensive production process. These improvements should be protected against unauthorized use.

Protecting information of this nature has its dangers, to be sure. The Minnesota Supreme Court perceptively acknowledged that a commercially superior process or device which is no more than a combination of known elements may, over time, become familiar to the trade as a whole through independent discovery, and conferring trade secret protection upon such information thus runs the risk of preventing former employees from using what had become over time common knowledge in the industry. But the court concluded that there was nothing to do but trust to the wisdom of the judge or jury trying the case to correctly determine the state of industry knowledge. This is clearly correct. There should be a place for the protection of mere cleverness in the framework of legal protection of proprietary information, both as a matter of policy and equity, and the possibility that a given case might be decided incorrectly is no reason not to make that effort.

PART THREE

Protecting
Proprietary
Information

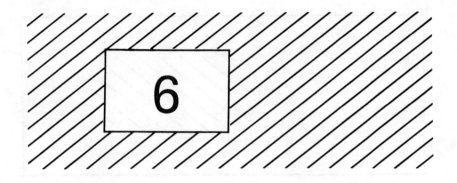

6

Secrecy and Security
Keeping Trade Secrets Secret

Secrecy, not surprisingly, is supposed to be fundamental to the concept of a trade secret. Many of the factors courts evaluate in assessing whether or not a trade secret exists—e.g., the nature and extent of security precautions, the value of the information, the ease or difficulty with which the information could be duplicated (see Chapter 2)—are directly related to the degree to which the purported trade secret is not known by others. This requirement of secrecy in fact has led to the general proposition that reasonable security precautions are a prerequisite to trade secret protection, on the rationale that if such measures have not been adopted or if voluntary disclosures have been tolerated, then the purported trade secret has most likely been disseminated and is no longer "secret." But the insistence on a reasonable measure of company security is also actuated, at least in part, by the attitude that a company cannot neglect to guard against the disclosure of its proprietary information and then expect a court to protect it from the consequences of its inaction. In one extreme expression of this perspective, a Michigan court asserted that secrecy does not even have an objective existence; information is secret "only to the extent that those who possess it choose to treat it so."

Although security is supposed to be a required antecedent of legal protection for proprietary information, it has not been an unreasonably burdensome requirement. Judges don't expect companies coming before them in trade secret cases to take heroic measures. They are interested only in assuring themselves that the measures adopted have been reasonable under the circumstances, or such as would make it difficult for others to discover the company's proprietary information without the use of improper means. However the standard might be verbalized, virtually any well-thought-out company security program will pass muster. Judges have consistently demonstrated a reluctance to substitute their judgment as to what security measures are appropriate for the judgment of the parties coming before them, so long as there has been a bona fide attempt by the company to keep its proprietary information secure. However, for some courts this means more than routine security measures that would be adopted by any company to keep out unwanted visitors.

But heroic security measures, while not necessarily mandated by the courts, can have strategic significance. Judges and juries dealing with an unfamiliar and arcane technology do not have the personal experience to assess whether an alleged trade secret really constitutes material information or not, or whether it is known by many others or not. They are only human, and if a company has elected expensive and elaborate security measures to protect its alleged trade secrets, it is inevitable that a judge or jury will be influenced by the extent of these precautions. If information so elaborately secured were not in fact valuable and secret, they would reason, why would the company go to all the trouble and expense of trying to prevent disclosure in the first place? It may in fact be the case that all the horses are already outside while the company is elaborately securing the stable; but it is much easier to prove the bolting of the door than the existence of the horses outside. Security measures can, as a practical matter, not only demonstrate that an alleged trade secret has been kept secure, but can also influence the decision as to whether a valuable secret existed in the first place.

Deciding What to Protect and How to Protect It

The objective of a company security program is to optimize protection, not maximize it. This has become almost a platitude. While a number of procedures and measures set forth in this section have been employed by companies that have successfully defended their trade secrets in court, it cannot be said that the best strategy information would be to adopt the greatest possible number of them. First of all, it would be prohibitively expensive. Moreover, by adopting security procedures to protect information manifestly not confidential in nature, a company might suggest to a judge that it really had no idea what it truly considered to be secret. Therefore, the first step in developing any company security program is to undertake an "information audit" and to make a deliberate decision as to what the company deems necessary or appropriate to protect from unauthorized disclosure.

When most people think of trade secret information, the first thing that comes to their minds are technical secrets. But the kinds of information in the possession of a company of any size extend well beyond the sphere of technology. A representative list of the kinds of information a company may wish to consider protecting against disclosure in one manner or another is set forth below. These categories are by no means exhaustive. Most companies not only have differing priorities as to each item, but also have categories of information requiring protection which are unique to them; for example, a licensing arrangement with a third party may require the institution of measures above and beyond what a company might have adopted on its own. Or particular types of information might be of particular interest to the competition, customers, suppliers, or the general public at a particular time. That is why no one can prescribe an information protection policy suitable for every company and for all time; the process must be performed internally, and continually, after due deliberation.

Types of Information Possibly Considered Proprietary[1]

1. Financial Information:
   Materials costs.
   Supplier discounts.
   Supplier identities.
   Overhead costs.
   Profit margins.
   Financing plans.
   Banking arrangements.

---

[1]See T. Walsh and R. Healey, *Protecting Your Business against Espionage* (New York: AMACOM, 1973), pp. 86–87, for another useful enumeration.

Present and future pricing policies.
Distributor and dealer discounts.
Identities of equity or debt holders.
Share holdings.
Capital contributions.
2. Organizational Information:
Opening and closing of facilities.
Number and type of employees per shift.
Equipment types and utilization rates.
Mergers.
Acquisitions.
Expansion plans.
Key employee acquisitions.
Key employee terminations.
Personnel information.
Transfers of key employees or functional groups.
3. Marketing Information:
New product developments.
Delivery schedules.
Product shortages or oversupply.
Customer lists.
Customer confidential information.
Identities of licensees.
Terms of licenses.
Market research and forecasts.
Contracts and contract negotiations.
New geographic or niche market penetration.
Marketing and advertising plans.
Marketing and advertising budgets.
4. Technical Information:
Plant organization and design.
Processes and methods of manufacture.
Machinery design and specifications.
Tolerance data.
The ingredients of materials.
The source of components.
Performance characteristics.
Service and repair records.
Scientific theorems.
Chemical formulas.
Software.
Research and development reports.
Research and development plans and objectives.
Research and development budgets.

Once it has been determined what information should be protected, the company then needs to identify each place *where* and how that information, in any form, reposes. Obviously it makes no sense to lock and guard research and development reports if a copy is freely available in a chronology file. Tracing the flow of information within the company in this manner may also suggest to senior management whether and to what extent confidential information is being too widely disseminated, whether access could be more narrowly circumscribed without adversely affecting the company's operations, and indeed whether protection for certain types of information is feasible at all.

There is no uniform set of rules by which to determine the proper distribution of information for every company. It is often the case that the decision as to how widely to distribute a document containing confidential information should be made either by the person who creates the document or by the person responsible for transmitting it. Although someone else could perform this function, the person who generated the information is the individual most capable of assessing its significance, and the person responsible for transmitting it is best able to contain its distribution. On the other hand, inexperience, want of judgment, or some other reason may mandate that these decisions be made by some other person. For extremely sensitive documents, it makes good sense to create a log to record distribution or make it company policy to restrict distribution to those identified on the documents themselves as having received a copy. Such a policy creates a trade secret "audit trail" in the event of a legal dispute, so that management can demonstrate with specificity precisely what proprietary information a given employee has had access to.

Particular attention should be directed to disseminating information beyond the walls, and the control, of the company. The professional staff should have at least a general understanding of what categories of information should never go out the door and under what circumstances other forms of sensitive information may be disclosed to proper parties. Because the flow of information to the outside world can assume protean forms, including correspondence and memoranda, professional papers, and communications with suppliers and customers, special care must be taken to ensure that confidential information is not inadvertently disclosed.

In addition to *identifying* the information to be maintained in confidence and *tracing* its dissemination within (and without) the company, it is also necessary to decide *how* these categories of information are to be protected, and from what. In any company, confidential information runs the gamut from the highly proprietary to the vaguely embarrassing, and obviously the same measures of protection are not appropriate to all.

Although some security specialists recommend "classifying" information the way the Pentagon does, this amounts to employing a bureaucratic bludgeon when a scalpel is called for. For example, even if a company regarded the financial arrangements of its most senior executives as having the same "confidentiality quotient" as the specifications for a certain proprietary process, most of the procedures applicable to the latter would be inapplicable to the former. If there is not some benefit to be derived from classification—such as a common set of security procedures for each classification level—then there is little reason to engage in the exercise. Also, classification tends to deflect attention from the specific reason for protecting any given category of information.

Once the objectives and procedures of a security program have been integrated into a specific recommendation, it is essential to then enlist the support of top management in its implementation. Security costs—not only money but time, effort, and aggravation. Without the will of senior management to guarantee its execution, a security program is doomed to failure. Middle-level managers will follow the example of their superiors in ignoring it, and the professional staff will come to regard the whole enterprise as a hypocritical exercise. And from a legal perspective, tolerating breaches of a security procedure may be worse than not adopting it in the first place. In a number of reported cases judges have taken a company's tolerance of security breaches as evidence that the company either did not regard the information as confidential at all, or that the company did not deserve the benefit of the court's injunctive powers because it had not itself taken the trouble to protect that information by enforcing its own confidentiality policy. Thus a modest program which is enforced is preferable to an elaborate body of rules which is steadfastly ignored.

Security also needs a constituency within the company in order to succeed. It has no natural constituency because security does not directly advance any of the basic objectives of a firm: profit generation, sales, growth, or asset preservation. Hence, good security has no natural tendency to advance careers, confer prestige, or contribute to the accumulation of influence. To create a constituency for company security, and the corporate culture to support it, security requires a corporate champion—someone who is not just responsible for security, but accountable for it. That person—who may certainly have other responsibilities in smaller organizations—must be granted the authority and resources to implement whatever policy management has adopted. He should report directly to a corporate officer, to assure that security lapses are brought to the attention of senior management promptly. In some corporations the security officer reports to the facilities manager or the director of personnel, but it is a better practice for security to be within the jurisdiction of the general counsel, or, even better, the vice president for finance. The CFO is by temperament sensitive to protecting company assets, and information is one of the most important assets a company has.

But like any set of rules, a security program cannot be imposed from above; it requires the consent of the governed. Unless the support of employees has been successfully elicited, the program cannot and will not succeed. If the company wants employees—particularly key technical and management employees with strong egos—to change their own behavior and to monitor the conduct of others, they have to know why, and they must be persuaded of its necessity. Without this kind of support, security procedures will only (a) cause annoyance and discontent, (b) encourage employees to look for less restrictive working environments, and (c) lead to mistakes because of employee unwillingness to follow established procedures to obtain needed information.

The means by which management can elicit employee support for the company's security program are varied. Companies have used letters from the president, statements of policy issued by the board of directors, discussions with supervisors, and more formal presentations to solicit employee support. Of course, whatever technique is adopted, the employees need to understand not only what security measures are to be applied to what information, but also why that information is regarded as confidential in the first place.

The truly successful security program will also seek to sensitize employees to the devious ways of an intensely competitive world, as, for example, how sensitive information might be extracted by a clever competitor (or indeed, a foreign agent) at professional conferences or trade shows. Other occasions upon which employees might inadvertently disclose highly confidential company information, such as employment interviews or sales presentations, should also be explored and the means for dealing with them discussed. For key employees, it is of particular importance that this training consist of more than passive observation, since (as every trial lawyer knows from hard experience) what a person says he understands and what in fact he has absorbed are often two very different things.

In some of the better-managed high-technology companies, security is not handed down from above. The staff doesn't just *learn* security policy—they *develop* it *themselves*. On new product development efforts, a security program is submitted to the company for approval along with the R&D program, the marketing plan, and the other facets of a new product release. When it is the employees themselves who have assembled the security program, security will inevitably be better enforced.

Representative Measures in Successful Company Security Programs

Although a company need adopt only *reasonable* security measures in order to invoke the powers of a court to prevent misappropriation of its proprietary information, what the law requires should not be the focus of a company's security program. The sole purpose of any security program should be to prevent a breach of security in the first place. The best trade secrets case is the one that never happened.

Representative measures employed by companies are enumerated below. Many of them will not be appropriate for a given company's circumstances, or will not be cost justified. Others will be inapplicable to the kinds of information a given company may feel compelled to safeguard. But the spectrum of enumerated measures should help to suggest to management procedures and alternatives that management may not have considered before.

1. Physical Security Measures

(a) Fences, barriers, and other physical restraints against unauthorized entry onto the premises.

(b) Guards, particularly to restrict access to sensitive areas and to record in logs the identity of persons entering the premises.

(c) Physical barriers around secret devices or processes or other physical segregation of such trade secrets to prevent access by the public and other employees.

2. Strategic Security Measures

(a) Maintenance of documents containing proprietary data in locked files or restricting access to files by placing the files in supervised areas; requiring that files be used in a protected area; and requiring that files be signed out before removal. Forms of electronic monitoring of files are available but expensive.

(b) Restricting access to copiers, particularly at night; using electronic keys so that the identity of the user can be traced; and requiring users to identify what was copied.

(c) The utilization of confidentiality stamps. A confidentiality notice serves both to identify what the company deems to be proprietary or confidential and to put the user on notice that his use is deemed to be in confidence.

(d) Escorting visitors on company premises. Under appropriate circumstances it may be advisable to record what a visitor observed in the way of equipment and processes, what documents he reviewed, and which persons he talked to. Confidentiality agreements should also be procured; a convenient procedure is to print the agreement on the application for a visitor's pass.

(e) Control of the manner in which sensitive documents are discarded.

(f) Locking up notebooks, data, and manuals when not in use; limiting the distribution and number of copies of such documents; and similarly restricting access to physical research materials and instruments.

(g) Not committing information to writing. In smaller firms, in particular, such information as experimentally derived constants or theories, process modifications, personnel evaluations of a sensitive nature, and market analyses often need not be written down because decision makers are assured of personal access to the possessors of the information at the time the information is needed. If information isn't written down, one of the principal avenues of unauthorized access to that information has been foreclosed.

(h) Procuring confidentiality agreements from third parties, such as manufacturers of equipment, customers in possession of proprietary material, and sales prospects. The nature of the confidentiality agreement will differ depending on the type of entity and its relationship with the company, of course, including the respective bargaining positions of the parties. Some components of the agreement might include a prohibition against copying of documents, an agreement not to disclose to the customer's own personnel except on a need-to-know basis; an agreement to procure confidentiality agreements from those further down the distribution chain; limitations on how or where the proprietary information is used and the conditions under which the information is to be returned; restrictions on disclosure of the nature or amount of goods purchased or fabricated; a stipulation by the customers not to reverse engineer the products sold; and, of course, an agreement not to use or disclose identified confidential information without prior written permission. And it's not enough just to write down what is to be done; there needs to be periodic audits to assure compliance.

(i) Physical dispersion of the steps in a proprietary process so that few employees are aware of the entire process. A company might even take the precaution of constructing or formulating components at different geographic locations. In addition, secret ingredients could be coded rather than identified, and component identification can be obliterated in the assembly process.

(j) Obliteration of identifying characteristics, part numbers, or manufacturer's identification of component parts before delivery to the customer.

(k) Documentation relating to company trade secrets, such as operating or training manuals, should be licensed or loaned to the customer, not distributed free of legal restrictions on use or disclosure.

3. Computer Security

(a) Restricting physical access to computer terminals and other peripheral devices.

(b) Placing computers, terminals, and other peripheral devices in secure locations under constant supervision.

(c) Using passwords, software "keys," and data encryption.

(d) Putting "fuses" into software to detect unauthorized access and to stop or erase the program if unauthorized access occurs.

(e) Using unusual formats for recording data.

(f) Imbedding firmware in a container or in material which is difficult to penetrate without damaging the firmware.[2]

---

[2] See M. R. Gilburne and R. L. Johnston, "The Protection and Enforcement of Trade Secrets in Software and High Technology Information," in *Intellectual Property Rights in High Technology Products and in Sensitive Business Information* (New York: Law and Business Inc./Harcourt Brace Jovanovich, 1982), for a more detailed discussion of this topic.

4. Employee Procedures

(a) Informing employees what is considered confidential prior to commencement of employment, keeping employees informed as categories of confidential information are added or deleted, enumerating what is considered confidential at employment termination, and extracting the employee's agreement to keep it confidential.

(b) Restricting employee access to areas where secret manufacturing processes or sensitive R&D is being conducted.

(c) Requiring employees to document R&D development so that a record of the information they had access to and the discoveries they participated in developing is readily available. These records will also serve to document the time and expense required for a new development (one of the factors evaluated by courts in assessing whether a trade secret exists).

(d) Adopting procedures to minimize, or at least to monitor, communications between the technical staff and sales personnel who may, without realizing it, disclose proprietary information.

(e) Directing employees to report all attempts by any unauthorized person to obtain proprietary company business information.

(f) Excluding disaffected employees from access to the most sensitive proprietary or confidential information of the company, and excluding terminating employees from access to any materials that might be of use to a competitor. Most employees who have given notice will not actually steal blueprints, specifications, program listings, or the like. But they generally regard it as fair to review for their own edification (and memory) material they had access to during their employment.

(g) Conducting an audit for each departing employee to ensure that he has returned all materials that might contain proprietary or confidential information and extracting from the employee a pledge that all such materials have in fact been returned.

(h) Taking special precautions with consultants. There is no quicker way to spread information throughout an industry than to give a consultant access to it. All consultants should be required to sign nondisclosure agreements. Moreover, a policy decision should be made beforehand as to what information a consultant should have access to, what information should be made available on request after evaluation by the company, and what information should not be made available under any circumstances.

Avoiding Common Pitfalls

No matter what size companies may be, or what industry they are in, they tend to make the same mistakes regarding the protection of proprietary information. Under the compulsion of common organizational influences and economic constraints, they fall into the same practices that have undone companies for decades. Addressing these pitfalls would go far toward guaranteeing the availability of judicial protection for their proprietary information.

Tours

In a trade secrets case filed by Motorola against Fairchild Instruments and Camera, it came to light that Motorola had taken customers on tours of its allegedly trade secret semiconductor production line. Motorola had also conducted a tour for one of its equipment manufacturers. It had even conducted tours for competitors' employees who were being recruited. And all this was done without requiring that confidentiality agreements be signed, without posting any signs warning that the details of the production line were considered proprietary, and without making any assertions of confidentiality prior to or during the tours. This degree of disclosure contributed mightily to the dismissal of Motorola's trade secret claims. And this is by no means the most extreme example. In a case arising in the textile industry, a company asserting that its manufacturing machinery and processes were trade secrets had actually conducted tours for its competitors! With facts like these, it is difficult for a company to plausibly maintain that it considered its production facilities to be secret and treated them as such.

Pride of ownership seems to impel managers to conduct tours of a company's facilities, but whether to give in to this impulse should be carefully evaluated beforehand. If there is some business purpose to be furthered by such a practice, whether it is technical in nature or merely a matter of public relations, the benefits may well outweigh the risks. However, even then tours need not be an all-or-nothing proposition. A company might well decide to allow tours but restrict them to designated areas; to maintain a significant distance between the visitor and a trade secret process, machine, or instrument; to place barriers around a certain segment of the production process; to restrict tours to specfied persons; or to require confidentiality agreements from visitors before a tour is conducted. And whatever limitations are adopted should be well documented and complied with. By such means the risk of disclosure of proprietary information—and the concomitant risk of a judicial finding of inadequate security—can be minimized.

Publicity and Promotion

Most commercial entities need promotion, and that entails communicating information about the company to the public. Publicity and promotion are not necessarily inconsistent with the demands of a company's information-protection policy, since a company usually need not disseminate trade secrets in order to further its promotional goals. But in a considerable number of cases companies have lost trade secret protection by disclosing a little bit too much about their products and processes during the course of promotional efforts. For example, in the *Motorola* case mentioned earlier, the company not only invited a trade journal to photograph its allegedly trade secret production line, but it also prepared a trade movie showing the production process.

Advertising has also served as the conduit whereby proprietary information has been inadvertently placed in the public domain. A manufacturer of laminated wood flooring, for example, was found to have disclosed its allegedly trade secret composition in the company's own advertising materials, while the manufacturer of a camera used for taking pictures of the cornea to fit contact lenses was found to have disclosed its alleged trade secrets in a catalog. In a variation on the same theme, a software house claiming that its list of customers was a trade secret was hard-pressed to explain why many of the companies it served were listed as representative clients in its advertising brochures.

Trade secret cases have also run aground on disclosures made at trade shows and professional conferences. Exhibiting allegedly proprietary machinery at trade shows has contributed to the loss of trade secret protection in a number of cases, and disclosures in conference papers and addresses have ruined several other trade secret claims. For example, in a software case a jewelry designer claiming as its trade secret a CAD/CAM system that controlled the engraving of molds for rings had permitted a conference presentation and the publication of a technical article that disclosed the very features it later claimed to be proprietary; indeed, an expert witness testified that from the article alone he could have duplicated the operations of the company's CAD/

CAM system. These disclosures substantially contributed to the adverse result.

These cases are unfortunate examples of what can happen out of inattention, lack of appreciation for the legal consequences of a company's conduct, and an absence of coordination between departments of a company. There are so many avenues by which proprietary information can be lost that only a diligent effort to identify these pathways and close them can succeed in preventing an inadvertent loss of confidential information. Such an effort need not impede the efforts of the marketing department or significantly curtail the participation of technical personnel in professional activities. In trade secret law, as in most other things, a little prevention is worth a lot of cure.

Restrictions on Dissemination to Employees

Some jurisdictions do not require employers to limit the disclosure of proprietary information among their employees on the rationale that employees have an implied duty to hold such disclosures in confidence. Other courts will often consider the degree of disclosure within the company in assessing whether secrecy has been adequately maintained. One oft-noted lapse has been the accessability of supposedly secret processes and machinery to employees who were not required to sign a confidentiality agreement. Another common error has been the failure of companies to advise employees as to the confidentiality of trade secrets to which they have access. And a few trade secret cases have failed on account of too-broad distribution of proprietary information within the company.

These kinds of oversights are entirely avoidable. Even a modest company security program should include confidentiality agreements directed to appropriate employees and properly identifying the nature of the company's proprietary information. A simple information audit will disclose whether proprietary information is being distributed too widely within the company.

Tolerating Breaches of Security

It was noted earlier that an unenforced security procedure is worse than not having adopted one in the first place. Let us put some flesh and blood on that theoretical proposition. In an Illinois decision the manufacturer of an ophthalmic camera alleged that it had strictly enforced a policy of confidentiality with respect to its camera. But only 8 out of 250 employees had ever heard of it! Moreover, the company had decided to monitor visitors to the plant, but then gave up trying to keep a visitor log. It should not be necessary to relate the outcome of this case. Loose security loses cases; it is like an open wound just waiting to be discovered by opposing counsel.

Selective enforcement of security measures is equally bad. As one court stated in ringing prose: "One may not venture on liberties with his own secret, may not lightly or voluntarily hazard its leakage or escape, and at the same time hold others to be completely obligated to observe it." Thus, when the former president of a polyethylene manufacturer had formed a competing company and utilized the trade secrets of his former company with the company's knowledge, the company's failure to respond foreclosed the company from enforcing its trade secrets later against anyone else as well.

The lesson to be drawn is that the courts won't tolerate "selective prosecution"; if a company permits unauthorized use or disclosure of company trade secrets, they won't be trade secrets anymore.

Dealing with the Issue of Public Sale

Once a company puts a product on the market, it obviously can no longer claim trade secret protection for any feature thereby disclosed. That certainly makes sense. If General Motors were to assert that an automobile's new aerodynamic design was a trade secret after the car had been displayed in showrooms across the country, the contention would rightly be met with laughter and ridicule.

The notion that all features of a product are disclosed when the product is sold is predicated on the commonsense assumption that what the public can see cannot be secret. But it is equally well recognized that public sale of a product will not be deemed to have disclosed the process by which the article was made, or the means of construction, or the tolerances for each of its parts, for the simple reason that one cannot ascertain this information from inspection of the product.

The difficult question is presented by the intermediate case: where certain types of information can be derived from a publicly-marketed product by reverse engineering (i.e., taking a product apart to see how it works), but only with considerable difficulty and at considerable expense. There is little uniformity in court decisions on this issue. An Illinois court ruled that the ingredients in tablets used to stain tooth plaque were not disclosed by public sale because the dyes, flavorings, and other components could only be determined by chemical analysis. However, under even more extreme facts, another court ruled that even though trade secrets embodied in the construction of industrial furnaces could only be determined upon inspection of an inoperative furnace, even though purchasers of such furnaces generally shut them down only once a year, and even though it would have taken three or four weeks to discover the trade secret aspects of the manufacturer's design, the trade secret features of the furnaces were disclosed on account of their public sale.

At any rate, a company need not assume that every trade secret associated with a new product will be lost when the product is marketed. Accordingly, the introduction of a new product calls for planning from a legal standpoint every bit as much as from the perspectives of the manufacturing and marketing departments. The first step in such a plan would be to withhold proprietary information disclosures until the last possible moment. Advance promotional material needs to be reviewed with an eye to this objective, and the company needs to consider what information to withhold from the sales staff. Disclosures to prospective buyers must be carefully controlled, and the use of confidentiality agreements seriously considered.

The next step is to analyze the product to determine what features will necessarily be disclosed by sale of the article on the open market. Even if the features of the product that make it proprietary will necessarily be disclosed by public sale, measures can still be taken to minimize the loss of proprietary information. For example, if specification or tolerance data would be essential or significantly helpful in reverse engineering the product, the company could withhold such information from its sales documentation, manuals, promotional material, and the like, or make it available only on a confidential basis. Technology also might be applied to make reverse engineering difficult or impracticable. Multiple bonding techniques might be employed or fragile parts encased in resin, epoxy, or some other suitable material to make access to the interior of a device more difficult.

The purpose of these precautions is not so much to foil reverse engineering as it is to prevent misappropriation of proprietary information by employees. It must be kept in mind that trade secret disputes usually arise when an ex-employee is alleged to have used company proprietary information acquired during the course of his employment. The employee will frequently invoke public sale to demonstrate that the information has ceased to be confidential and that he is therefore no longer under a legal duty not to use it. If reverse engineering can be rendered sufficiently difficult, costly, and time-consuming, courts may well be inclined to accept the proposition that proprietary features have not become public knowledge by public sale.

Under certain circumstances, a sale may be structured to preclude public disclosure at all. For example, sales of systems or large units of equipment may be conditioned on a confidentiality agreement and a commitment by the purchaser to take elaborate precautions to prevent public access. Or if company trade secrets are embodied in the documentation which accompanies a sale, the contract of sale could include a confidentiality agreement barring disclosure of the documentation outside the company and restricting access within the company to identified employees. Although confidentiality agreements may not be appropriate for mass-marketed products, their use in association with the public distribution of goods has been held to preserve the confidentiality of information disclosed by the sale of a fairly large number of units. For example, when Data General gave out, under a confidentiality agreement, design drawings of its popular Nova computer to thousands of purchasers, the judge ruled that even such broad distribution did not constitute general public disclosure.

The Mixed Blessings of Patent Protection

When most people think about protecting inventions, they think of patents. A patent confers the right to exclude others from use of a discovery for 17 years. But there is an associated cost: full and complete disclosure of the discovery. This is the trade-off: the inventor discloses his invention to the world, thereby adding to the fund of human knowledge and stimulating further discoveries; in return, he receives a monopoly for a set duration of time. But in a world where product life cycles often run closer to 17 months than 17 years, the cost of patent protection may not be worth the price. For products with short life cycles, a company may well be better off relying on trade secret protection and not disclosing the discovery to anyone. In this manner a trade secret can be maintained indefinitely; the classic example is the formula for Coca Cola.

There are risks associated with this strategy, of course. Trade secret protection safeguards only against improper use or disclo-sure. If someone were to discover a company's trade secret inde-pendently, he could use it with impunity or disclose it to the world and destroy the secret all together.

But a patent has its own perils. Patents are expensive. They take years to be approved. And worst of all, once a patent appli-cation is granted, the patent description becomes public knowl-edge. If someone later challenges the patent before the Patent and Trademark Office or in court and the patent is invalidated, not only will patent protection be lost, but trade secret protec-tion will have become unavailable on account of the public dis-closure of the patent upon issuance.

Nor is the risk of invalidation the only cause for worry. Once a valuable patent issues, the patent holder can assume that one of three things will ensue: (a) the patent will suggest new ideas to competitors, leading to an even better discovery; (b) others will try to use information from the patent without infringing the pat-ent itself ("inventing around" the patent); or (c) the patent will simply be infringed.

Infringement is a commercial fact of life. This may not be in accordance with the theory underlying the patent laws; they are supposed to protect against the use, manufacture, or sale of one's invention. But theory somehow has a way of getting lost in the harsher world of legal and economic realities.

Distinguishing between infringement and mere invention around a patent can become an almost metaphysical inquiry, and infringement may be very difficult to establish. About half the cases in which patents have been adjudged valid also resulted in a finding of no infringement. Moreover, patent litigation is ex-pensive; legal fees in six figures are not uncommon.

Even where infringement is clear, the patent holder can expect the infringer to assert that the patent is invalid, and the track record of patents in federal court is not good. Studies conducted at various times over the past 30 years show that about three out of five patents litigated to judgment are declared invalid, and in certain areas of the country that figure rises to three out of four. These are not good odds. Even though these statistics may im-prove now that a special court has been established to hear all patent appeals, the uncertainties associated with patent litiga-tion are nonetheless real and continuing.

Even worse, for many companies, and particularly for the small entrepreneurial firm, patent litigation may be a no-win proposition. The company will often have expended consider-able sums in research to develop its patent or to purchase the rights to a patent. These costs must be recovered in the price charged for the invention in order for the discovery to be profitable. But patent infringers are not under the same economic constraints. They have no R&D costs to amortize, and they can undercut the patent holder's price and force him to sell at a loss or at least at an insufficient profit at the same time he is trying to conduct costly patent litigation. If the firm is in need of additional capital on account of these problems, it will find the capital markets unsympathetic to the prospect of protracted and expensive patent litigation and the prospect of red ink on the company's books.

What's more, the patent holder may never even learn that his patent is being infringed. There is no police force in the marketplace enforcing the patent laws; the patent holder has to do it himself. This can be a time-consuming and expensive proposition. If the infringement occurs in an area geographically remote from the patent holder, or technologically remote from the patent holder's own industry, the infringement may never be discovered.

Nor are the hazards of patent protection limited to litigation risks. A company may determine that it will seek a patent for part of its proprietary technology and keep the remainder secret. For example, a company might patent an article but not the process by which it is made. But out of carelessness or because it is necessary in order to make a patent intelligible (a prerequisite to issuance of a patent), so much of the information sought to be concealed may have to be disclosed or suggested in the patent that its secrecy may be irrevocably compromised.[3]

Once again, the best way to resolve the dilemma of patent versus trade secret protection is to anticipate it and to develop a strategy to minimize exposure and expense. But for the reasons set forth in this section, companies should at least consider alternatives to patent protection. A patent may well be the best alternative, but again, it may not be; and he who patents in haste may repent at leisure.

A Postscript or Prologue on Secrecy and Security

A few years ago, a manufacturer of hickory flavoring (liquid smoke) brought suit against a former employee alleging misap-

---

[3]For another discussion, see Philip Sperber, *Intellectual Property Management* (New York: Clark Boardman, Ltd., 1982).

propriation of its manufacturing trade secrets. The only issue in the case was the adequacy of the company's security. The evidence disclosed that the company did not admonish all its employees as to the secrecy of its process and that numerous employees possessed information about the manufacturing process. Moreover, although the plant was surrounded by a fence, the gates were left unguarded and the employees were not required to wear any identification. In another case, a manufacturer of voting machines had distributed allegedly secret technical drawings and blueprints to two and perhaps three companies without any restriction on their use, and all employees had free access to the documents. Yet in each of these cases trade secrets were found to exist nonetheless.

One might reasonably wonder about these decisions. If, as so many decisions have traditionally assumed, both security measures and secrecy in fact are required for the recognition of a trade secret, then these decisions don't make sense. They could be dismissed as mere aberrations, but that would be too easy an answer; for as will be seen below, there are too many decisions of a like character.

What emerges from reading this section is the distinct impression that secrecy and security aren't *really* prerequisites of trade secret protection at all. Courts have favored any number of reasons to overlook not only lapses in security (or no security at all) but even a demonstrable want of secrecy, in order to prevent inequities or inequitable conduct. Let us consider a few of them:

The Faithless Employee Exception

A software house in Pennsylvania had written a computer program to process magazine subscription lists for the purpose of determining which subscribers had recently moved, so that client stores in the vicinity could send targeted advertising. One of its clients, apprehensive as to the company's financial stability, told an employee of the company to procure a backup copy of the programs to use in the event that the software house went out of business. The employee did so without informing the company, and the client then hired the employee as a consultant, terminated the company's services, and used the software to develop new programs to perform the same service. The facts were thus fairly egregious; the software house was victimized both by an unfaithful employee and by a duplicitous client. When it sued its former client for misappropriating trade secrets, the client asserted that the company had no trade secrets because it had not adopted adequate security measures. But the court, obviously galled by the client's conduct, ruled (allegations of inadequate security not withstanding) that the software company could reasonably assume "that its employees and officers would abide by their obligation not to disclose its trade secrets...." The implication of this position is that security measures are not necessary if employees are under an obligation not to disclose confidential information.

The "Purloined Letter" Exception

A number of years ago, the manufacture of oxygen breathing hose was dominated by one company, whose process for making the hose resulted in a substantially superior product.

Not knowing a good thing when they had it, the company did little to protect the secrecy of its process. One of its suppliers was given the run of the plant, but was not required to sign a confidentiality agreement. The company ran tours of the plant. The company demonstrated its production process for a trade group. Workers were permitted to have visitors on the plant floor. The plant's garage doors to the street were left open.

An invitation like that was too good to pass up; the aforementioned supplier, who had learned the process well enough to duplicate it, did. Was trade secret protection deemed lost on account of inadequate security measures? Perish the thought. Said the court: "in its particular community and environment, it may well be that [the company] considered that too elaborate efforts at concealment would call attention to what was being concealed..." The case is not an anomaly; there are others of a like tenor.

The Incomplete Disclosure Exception

Sometimes judges will overlook voluntary disclosures of trade secret information by resorting to the explanation that the disclosure was incomplete and did not reveal the trade secret in its entirety. For example, in one case a research engineer working for a manufacturer of precision scales went into business for himself in competition with his former employer and hired a draftsman formerly employed by the company to draw from memory a set of parts drawings for the scale. When the company sued, the engineer responded with evidence that the company had actually shown parts drawings to sales prospects. But this voluntary disclosure of material that supposedly embodied trade secrets was cavalierly dismissed with the comment that the drawings had revealed only the external features of the company's product.

The Probable Use Exception

In the ordinary trade secret case, a company's security measures are compared against the company's security lapses, and some assessment is made as to whether the secrecy of the alleged trade secret has been maintained. The problem with this process is that it occurs in a vacuum. How is it possible, for example, to assess whether security precautions are adequate without knowing what they are supposed to be adequate *for*? Does the objective of security toward which the law strives mean security from disclosure to the general public? To the industry? To a single person?

A number of courts have implicitly rejected the traditional disembodied assessment of security measures in favor of a much more focused and pragmatic test: whether the security procedures adopted were likely to conceal a purported trade secret from access by someone in a position to actually use it. One of the most emphatic statements of this position appears in a New Jersey case involving secret chemical processes. The defendant, a chemist who had appropriated the processes, asserted that the director of the lab had had numerous conversations concerning the processes in public places where they might have been overheard and therefore that security had been breached and secrecy no longer existed. But the court expressed its doubt that these arcane discussions could have been heard or understood by passersby, even assuming they were interested.

In essence the court was asserting that security per se was not the issue. Instead, the relevant inquiry was perceived to be whether, given company security measures (or a lack of them), trade secret information could be expected to have passed outside the company in some usable form.

Similar sentiments are expressed in another well-known trade secret case, where employees of a shoe manufacturer formed a competing company and appropriated secret features of their former employer's proprietary machine. Even though it was shown that persons outside the company had access to the machine and had been permitted to observe it in operation, the court discounted this disclosure with the observation that "there was no evidence that any of these persons interested himself sufficiently to learn the details of the construction and operation of the machine so as to reproduce it."

Indeed, some cases appear to assume that if disclosures by the owner of a trade secret do not render the information accessible to a *competitor*, the information continues to maintain its status as a trade secret. When an employee of a ski manufacturer terminated his employment and joined a competitor, he utilized the manufacturing procedures he had learned in his former employment, and his former employer sought an injunction against his use of its ski manufacturing trade secrets. The employee contended that everything asserted to be a trade secret had been disclosed by tours of the company's facility and by disclosure of a cross-section of its ski at a trade show. The court dismissed the first contention with the comment that competitors had not been permitted to view the company's manufacturing operation. And the display of its trade secret methods of manufacture at a trade show were dismissed with the comment that no competitor had been present!

Disclosure for a Limited Purpose

At the turn of the century, a manufacturer of railway equipment sent blueprints to prospective purchasers to enable them to ascertain whether its railcars were suitable for their use. The manufacturer also provided copies of blueprints to purchasers so that they could inspect the cars, and, after delivery, order parts and make repairs. Several railroads delivered these drawings to a competitor, which commenced manufacture using them. Despite the lack of any restriction on the use of the blueprints, the Pennsylvania Supreme Court prohibited the use of the drawings by a rival company on the rationale that "the purpose for which they were delivered by the plaintiff was understood by all parties."

It is hard to reconcile this case, which embodies a doctrine— referred to here as "disclosure for a limited purpose"—with a requirement of "secrecy," or even with a requirement of "reasonable" security. With such wide distribution, continuing to call such information "secret"—whether it is termed "qualified secrecy," "reasonable secrecy," "relative secrecy," or anything else—distorts the word beyond all meaning. But one frequently finds judges willing to invoke the "limited purpose" doctrine to excuse an unqualified disclosure of the supposed secret to third parties. For example, in one case where the design of cup-making machinery was asserted to be a trade secret, the judge dismissed the fact that the owner had sent blueprints to suppliers without any pledge of confidentiality by saying the suppliers were reputable companies that could be trusted to maintain their confidentiality—without indicating where the supposed duty of confidentiality came from. In another case an Arizona court upheld as a trade secret a chemical formula for solutions used to clean printing press machinery, despite the fact that the formula had been disclosed to other firms pursuant to licensing agreements which contained no apparent limitation on disclosure or use. Similarly, a New York court ruled that the design of an aircraft armament storage and control system continued to be a trade secret even though the company that developed it had prepared a brochure describing the system's functions and mode of operation and then distributed it to military bases, government agencies, and various private companies for the "limited purpose"(!) of promoting the sale of the system.

Admittedly, these decisions do not represent a new consensus. Many trade secret decisions continue to reflect the traditional rule that disclosure—sometimes even a single disclosure—of allegedly trade secret materials, such as blueprints or operating manuals, place the information contained in them in the public domain, outside of the realm of the secret and confidential. But what these decisions apparently *do* represent is a serious undercurrent of dissatisfaction with the mainstream of trade secret law, which would permit the duplicitous disclosure or use of proprietary information to go unpunished because of the fortuitous circumstance that inadequate security measures were implemented by the originator, or voluntary good faith disclosures were excessive. And this disquiet can only increase in an economy in which information is as much a repository of economic value as money, stock, and other forms of capital. Such an economic system must have the ability to accommodate the sale and exchange of information without fear that disclosure will result in the loss of rights in the information.

Trade Secret Misappropriation or Breach of Confidence?

At this juncture, let us glance backward momentarily. We have seen that the traditional conception of *trade secrets* has been as a subset of the universe of secrets. We have also observed that in assessing whether a trade secret exists, courts have looked to the degree to which the information constituting an alleged trade secret is already commonly known and to the security precautions taken to prevent the dissemination of the information and the accompanying loss of secrecy. Finally, we have noted that when a party has had its proprietary information used by another but has not taken very extensive measures to prevent unauthorized access to the information, judges often fashion exceptions to the requirement of secrecy and security in order to reach an equitable result. In the process, the notion of secrecy has suffered.

Let us now consider for a moment a different set of circumstances where there is broad public distribution of products and services embodying proprietary information, but only under a contractual pledge of confidentiality. Disclosures in confidence have usually not been regarded as constituting a breach of security and a waiver of secrecy. But what about wide public distribution? For example, it was asserted in one case that payroll software that had been distributed to 600 customers, albeit under a confidentiality agreement, was no longer secret on account of the breadth of disclosure. But the court disagreed.

Yet if information can remain a trade secret despite distribution to 600 persons, then how about disclosure to 6,000? When Data General began selling its Nova 1200 minicomputer, it offered its customers the circuit drawings so that they could perform their own maintenance. These drawings were disclosed under a confidentiality agreement. When another company procured the drawings and produced its own knock-off version, Data General sued. The imitator's defense was that the drawings had been so widely distributed that they were no longer in any sense secret and that 6,000 persons had had access to the drawings. But the design drawings were nonetheless held to be trade secrets, and their use by the imitator was enjoined.

And a program to help smokers quit smoking was held to remain a trade secret despite the untold hundreds of persons nationwide who had attended the program and so were aware of its contents—again, because the attendees had each signed confidentiality agreements.

If disclosure of this magnitude under a pledge of confidence does not destroy the "secrecy" of a trade secret, trade secret law would seem not to be about secrecy at all, but rather about confidentiality, and about the obligation to maintain confidential relationships.

In fact, quite a number of jurisdictions have adopted precisely that perspective, and have prohibited the unauthorized use of information disclosed in confidence whether the information was really confidential in fact or not. For example, in the early days of containerized shipping, a manufacturer of containers disclosed in confidence, during the course of negotiations for the sale of the business, all of the engineering details of the container design. The defendant then broke off negotiations and began manufacturing similar containers, and was so successful that the first company was driven out of business. Though the defendant had obtained the design information in confidence during the negotiations, it turned out that all of the design information *could* have been obtained by inspecting containers sold to others. The design information was thus freely available to anyone and everyone who cared to discover it. Nonetheless the court ruled that the fact that the design could have been obtained by inspection was irrelevant because it had not been so acquired in fact. Not only were damages awarded, but an injunction was entered against defendant's further manufacture of shipping containers embodying the pilfered design.

This may seem at first glance a somewhat startling conclusion. In essence, it means that publicly available information can be disclosed in confidence, which seems almost a contradiction in terms. The rationale advanced for this proposition was that public policy favors proper methods of business conduct in commercial transactions. Bleeding someone of information during the course of negotiations for the sale of a business, and then discarding that party and commencing competition with him using the information he disclosed, was not regarded as comporting with appropriate standards of business conduct. A basic policy decision had been made; commercial fairness warranted placing restrictions on the use of public domain information.

There are many similar cases. For example, in one decision, an engineer demonstrated a new design for a weed eater (a device that spun a nylon monofilament at high speed and cut down weeds, grass, and underbrush) to a company interested in purchasing it. But the company thought the engineer was asking far too much, so it designed and sold a similar device. When the engineer sued, the company contended that the device was not a trade secret because its design would be disclosed upon sale. But the fact that the company *could* have obtained the design information properly did not matter, since it did in fact obtain the design under the cloak of a confidentiality agreement and then violated the agreement.

The same rationale has also been applied to information acquired by employees during the course of their employment. An employee of a chemical company who had signed a confidentiality agreement and then began competing with his former employer was found to have breached his fiduciary obligations to his former employer, even though the chemical formulas he used were generally known in the trade, or could have been ascertained by chemical analysis. Because the employee had obtained such information in the course of a confidential relationship (his employment), rather than from publicly available sources, he was enjoined from using the formulas.

Or take an example in the business-information context. The former president of an industrial laundry service was enjoined in one case from competing with his former company for one year on account of his knowledge of confidential customer data obtained during his previous employment. Even though much of the information in his possession concerning the requirements and preferences of the company's customers might have been known by competitors, the relevant inquiry was stated to be not how others *could* have acquired the data but how the defendant *had* done so. Since the customer data was obtained in the course of his employment relationship, it was not permissible for him to use this information to the detriment of his former employer.

An Information Policy for an Information Society

There are scores of cases like those described in the previous section, where the courts have, in essence, discarded the requirement that, to be protectable against unauthorized use, information disclosed in confidence must really *be* confidential. These cases represent a basic policy decision that it is more important to deter dishonesty in business transactions and to encourage commercial fairness than it is to keep the use of public domain information free of all restrictions.

Certainly promoting business morality is an important policy; but United States Supreme Court decisions in the patent arena have suggested that the policy in favor of unfettered use of public domain information is paramount. Subscribing to this view, a few courts have held that the enforcement of an agreement not to disclose, or to pay royalties for the use of, know-how which is not (or is no longer) secret is contrary to public policy and void. To enforce such an agreement, the argument goes, would conflict with the policy of the patent laws to promote the use of information in the public domain. The specter to be guarded against is well expressed in a New Jersey federal court decision:

> A duty not to use an idea already known cannot be created by virtue of the fact that one makes a confidential disclosure of that idea... If the rule were not so restricted it is obvious that by dis-

closing an idea under delusions of confidence, the person making the disclosure thereafter could prevent the confidante from subsequently making use of it, even though the idea was well known prior to the date of the disclosure and open to the use of all others in the world.

If this was the law, said another court, "the monopoly of the patent law would be extended with disastrous effect."

This kind of thinking utterly misconceives the role of information in an information economy. "Public" information can retain real economic value notwithstanding its public availability. A good example to illustrate this point is presented by an Oregon case concerning the design of a garbage truck. The plaintiff had, after long design work, hit upon a truck body that resulted in more effective compaction of garbage. However, unknown to him, the same design had been arrived at years before, and similar truck bodies were in use elsewhere *throughout the country.* The manufacture of the bodies had been contracted out, and when the orders started pouring in, the contractor went into competition with the designer, pilfering his design. When the designer sued, asserting that the manufacturer was in breach of confidence, the manufacturer responded that there was nothing to be in breach of confidence *of,* since the design information was well known throughout the country. Perhaps so, said the Oregon Supreme Court, but *not* in Oregon: "The fact that the idea was already developed by others at the time of disclosure may make it less valuable in the market. Yet the information or knowledge may give to the possessor commercial advantage over his competitors." The public nature of the information might have *reduced* its value, but certainly had not *eliminated* its value. The "secret" and the "public" lie along a continuum, and as long as someone is willing to pay for information, its public nature has obviously not entirely deprived it of value.

It is by now a platitude to say that we are in the midst of an information explosion of unprecedented magnitude. It is the task of an ever-growing segment of the economy to access, organize, and utilize information which for the most part is in the public domain. But the fact that information is—in a technical sense— "public" knowledge should not compromise the confidentiality of that information as accessed and organized, if it is communicated under a pledge of confidence.

It must be kept in mind that the public domain is not a place, like a library, where one can go to look up technical or trade information. Finding or acquiring commercially usable information from the public domain is often a "needle-in-the-hay-stack" proposition in multiple dimensions. One has to have the background to know where to look, the experience to know what to look for, the judgment to know how to differentiate between the relevant and the irrelevant, and the education to understand it all. The location, organization, and provision of information has added value even if the underlying information is "public." Therefore, an agreement to hold in confidence embodiments of even publicly available information should be enforced where this screening function has been performed.

There is nothing radical in the proposition that courts should enforce agreements the subject matter of which is a product or service which merely represents the efficient packaging of public domain information; indeed, that is precisely what a service economy is all about. As the California Supreme Court has noted: "The lawyer or doctor who applies specialized knowledge to a state of facts and gives advice for a fee is selling and conveying an idea. In doing that he is rendering a service. The lawyer and doctor have no property rights in their ideas as such . . . but . . . the law does not hesitate to infer or imply a promise to compensate for it."

For a number of years several leading jurisdictions have enforced contracts to pay for ideas which were not novel, secret, or confidential in any way. As one well-known example, consider the case of a producer who hit upon the idea of casting Richard Burton and Elizabeth Taylor as the protagonists in Shakespeare's *The Taming of the Shrew*, with Franco Zefferelli as the director. The movie was made, but without the participation of the producer who originated the idea, and he sued. Despite his acknowledgment that there was nothing unique in the idea of bringing a Shakespeare play to the screen or even of making a movie of *The Taming of the Shrew* specifically, or in using two well-known actors, or in using a stage director to direct a motion picture, the court held that if those benefiting by the producer's idea had agreed to pay him for use of the idea, he should recover even if there was nothing about his idea that was not in the public domain.

There is no reason why information in any form—be it an idea, professional experience, a design, or a process—should not be treated in the same manner. And if an agreement to pay for public domain ideas and information is enforceable, then so should a promise by a purchaser of such information not to disclose it to others. The United States Supreme Court acknowledged that proposition many years ago in *Chicago Board of Trade v. Christie Grain and Stock Co.*

The Board of Trade, a commodities exchange, delivered price quotes to telegraph companies who then communicated the quotes to those who had entered into a contract with the Board of Trade promising not to disclose the price quotes to others. A company induced one of the recipients of this information to breach its confidentiality pledge, and commenced selling the price quotes itself. It could hardly be said that there was anything secret about the prices at which commodities were being sold on one of the largest commodity trading floors in the world. But the price quotations, revealed under a pledge that they not be disclosed to others, were protected against unauthorized use nonetheless.

Packagers of information should have the fruits of their labors protected every bit as much as the originators of information do. They have a vital role to play in an information economy, akin to the role played by brokers in a capitalist economy. Failing to provide protection to the product of their efforts would create a substantial economic disincentive to the efficient packaging and dissemination of information. This would, in turn, have an adverse impact on productivity, for an information economy requires that information be freely transferrable and able to be put to its most productive use, just as a capitalist economy requires that capital be put to *its* most productive use. If information merchants cannot rely on legal protection for their "product," they will adopt strategies to sell the benefits and incidents of information rather than the information itself. This would inevitably be of less use to the purchaser, who would be in the best position to put the knowledge and information to its most productive use. Indeed, at the extreme the failure to provide adequate legal protection might result in the decision not to incur the cost of assembling the information in the first place. Entities in the business of assembling information need to know that if they disclose information in confidence, they cannot be dispossessed of their rights in that information by a later claim that the information actually came from the public domain.

Obviously, this argument cannot be extended to relations between employers and employees, for to enforce a confidentiality agreement as to information not confidential in fact would dispossess the employee of the benefit of his employment experience, and generally lead to the untoward consequences discussed at length in Chapter 4. But between companies acting at arms length, a promise should be a promise—not on account of the sanctity of contracts or out of a fine moral sense, but because it is wise public policy to enforce such agreements.

The Defensive Use of Security Programs:
Deciding What *Not* to Protect

As was mentioned earlier, developing a security program has, as one of its objectives, the determination of what not to protect since there are costs associated with any security measure, and one needs to be assured that the cost is worth the benefit. But there is a strategic, as well as an economic, rationale for the non-protection of certain categories of information. Cases are legion where a company carefully sought to maintain the secrecy and security of a machine, process, or the like which it was then sued for misappropriating. Having by its conduct ratified the proposition that the device or process was in fact secret (why maintain security otherwise?), the company was effectively foreclosed from arguing to the contrary in the lawsuit filed against it.

Indeed, the effect of protecting information later claimed to have been misappropriated can be severe. In one instance, where the developer of a process for case-hardening steel induced a financial backer to enter into a joint venture with him by representing that his process was secret, the court refused to consider the developer's contention, in a subsequent trade secret lawsuit against him by the financial backer, that the process really was not secret after all. On account of the representations made as to the secrecy of the process, the court ruled the developer of the process estopped (i.e., legally foreclosed) from taking a legal position that contradicted his earlier representations.

Not all courts are so draconian. Indeed, one court said the fact that a company treated research and development information as confidential was "remote and insignificant" to a determination whether such information was in fact confidential. But even if a judge does not treat a company's efforts to maintain the secrecy of certain information as dispositive on the issue of the secrecy and confidentiality of that information, the circumstance would at least constitute an implicit admission that would be a very powerful piece of evidence and would make a company's contention to the contrary hard to sustain.

The same principle applies to representations by the marketing and sales staff. In case after case one finds that an employee of a company sued for trade secret misappropriation has been out proclaiming to the world the uniqueness, secrecy, or superiority of the product or process claimed to have been misappropriated; and the outcome has been predictably adverse.

Trade secret litigation is difficult enough without shooting your own foot off. Just a little planning and a little communication are all that's necessary to avoid doing a trade secret opponent's work for him.

First, when a company becomes aware of the assertion that certain information in its possession is proprietary to another, the matter should be communicated to the various line officers within the company, from manufacturing to marketing. Such knowledge may come to the company by way of contact from a competitor or a competitor's attorney, from discussions with a newly recruited employee, through information obtained in the course of the licensing of proprietary technology from another entity, or simply from the word on the street. Many of these claims may either by undisputed, on the one hand, or frivolous, on the other, and may not warrant discussion. But the heads of the operating departments should at least be aware of what the outside world is claiming as trade secrets.

Second, if a claim ever matures into an actual dispute, the company should devote attention to it on an interdisciplinary basis. The merits of the claim need to be discussed and debated, and the counsel of the company's lawyer should be communicated to the company's department heads. This way, if the company decides to respond, at least everyone will be aware of its position, and no one will be unknowingly undermining it.

Here is one final suggestion for companies with the resources to afford it. Most large and many medium-sized corporations are familiar with antitrust compliance programs, designed both to discover potentially unfavorable evidence before it is unearthed in a lawsuit and to prevent untoward antitrust disasters from happening in the first place. A company may decide to devote some of its security resources to detection and avoidance of exposure in proprietary information matters in a like manner.

Confidentiality and Invention Assignment Agreements
What They Are, What They're For, and What to Look Out For

In former years, employment agreements containing confidentiality clauses and patent and invention assignment provisions were less common. Companies tended to rely on patent protection, and on the allegiance of employees and the threat of an adverse job recommendation, to prevent the misappropriation of trade secrets. Only the larger, more sophisticated companies were familiar with trade secret protection, and with the use of contractual arrangements to protect proprietary information. But with the enhanced role that information plays in a technological economy, and with the increasing sophistication of managers, the use of confidentiality and invention assignment agreements is now routine in many industries.

As used in the present context, a confidentiality agreement is simply a contract between a company and its employee whereby the employee agrees to keep confidential and not to disclose or use the company's proprietary information. Patent and discovery assignment agreements are usually contained in the same employment agreement. They provide, in substance, for the assignment (i.e., transfer) of all rights the employee may hold with respect to inventions or discoveries which he developed during the course of employment.

Confidentiality Agreements

Why They Are Necessary

Since the misappropriation of trade secrets and confidential business information by an employee is prohibited by law whether there is a contractual prohibition or not, one might wonder why it is necessary to go through all the trouble of drafting a confidentiality agreement and instituting procedures to have it signed by a firm's employees.

The answer is grounded in the practicalities of trade secret litigation, rather than in legal doctrine. In most disputes between companies and their former employees over rights in information, the central issue is whether the information was secret or confidential in the first place. If the information—whether it be a formula, a process, a design, or whatever—could not be so characterized, an employee may use it with impunity. As was discussed in Chapter 4, simply because an employee acquires information from his employer in the course of his employment does not mean that information will necessarily be regarded as confidential. Information that is the natural product of a given employment activity, and which would be acquired by any person similarly employed, is not proprietary information.

But assessing whether information is a natural product of employment, or is instead proprietary to the company, can be an exceedingly difficult task for judge or jury—particularly when the information concerns an unfamiliar and complex technology. In such circumstances, it would be natural to seek guidance from the parties themselves as to what they conceived to be proprietary at the inception of the employment relationship. The confidentiality agreement is specifically addressed to this issue, and such an agreement can provide at least general guidance as to what the parties originally thought concerning this matter.

A second reason for using confidentiality agreements arises when an employment contract is contemplated for other reasons.

For example, a company hiring a key executive or an especially talented engineer may have to negotiate an employment agreement fixing a term of guaranteed employment, setting forth the terms under which bonuses are to be paid, obligating the company to issue stock options, and so forth. A comprehensive employment contract covering many aspects of the employment relationship, but failing to deal with the subject of confidentiality, could be construed to constitute the entire agreement between the parties. This interpretation would preclude the finding of an implicit agreement that information received by the employee would be held in confidence. There are defects in this reasoning, it must be acknowledged. If confidential information is protected by operation of law whether or not there is a contractual agreement to that effect, it may seem strained to assert that the absence of a confidentiality provision in an employment contract amounts to an abandonment of common-law protection. But courts have in fact employed just such a legal analysis on occasion. Moreover, in light of the prevalent use of confidentiality agreements today, a judge is going to look with considerable suspicion on trade secret claims where there is an elaborate employment contract but no mention anywhere of the confidentiality of company information. Since there is a built-in judicial hostility to restraints on employee mobility, there is simply no justification for such a glaring omission if a company is serious about protecting its proprietary information from disclosure.

The absence of a written confidentiality agreement can be used to the disadvantage of the employer in other ways as well. For example, in one case the fact that a process for making pressure seals was known by numerous employees who had not been required to sign confidentiality agreements was cited as an example of inadequate security. This contributed to the judge's conclusion that the process was not in fact secret in the first place. So not having a confidentiality agreement is not merely a matter of a lost opportunity; this circumstance can also be used offensively against the company in any trade secret dispute in which it becomes involved.

In smaller companies and particularly in start-ups, where everyone knows each other, there is an understandable disinclination to compel all employees to confirm that they will not misappropriate company proprietary information. Such companies operate informally, and management and employees may resent both the formality a nondisclosure agreement represents and the mistrust such a procedure implies. But this informality can have some unanticipated results. It is not just that recollections are likely to differ in the event of a dispute many years later; in addition, in the absence of a written document, a judge must interpret events in accordance with his own perceptions. This can lead to some surprises. For example, when an employee hired by a company to develop rocket valves and components was tendered an agreement to assign all his inventions to the company, he was orally instructed that the company was the sole owner of the designs and that the designs were not to be shown to any competitors or used after termination of employment. Because the employee failed to indicate that he agreed with these terms, the court therefore concluded that he *disagreed*, and therefore that he was not bound by these oral injunctions! Admittedly, this example is selected more for effect than for its typicality, but it does illustrate the diverse ways in which a dispute over the use of proprietary information can go awry absent an effective written confidentiality agreement.

A confidentiality agreement confers other benefits as well. In any trade secret dispute between a company and former employees, the judge will be unfamiliar with any of the parties, the facts, and even the technology. He will want to be reassured that the company is not using his court to oppress its former employees or to suppress legitimate competition. An employee confidentiality agreement can provide such assurances in a variety of ways. First, it demonstrates that the protection of proprietary information is a long-standing company policy that has been pursued in a systematic way—not an afterthought when a valued employee has left for the competition. Second, an employee's signature on a confidentiality agreement signifies at the very least that the employee has been put on notice that he occupies a position of trust and confidence and that he may become privy to company trade secrets. He may dispute that particular categories of information are in fact secret, but he cannot assert that no confidential relationship existed between himself and his employer. Third, a written confidentiality agreement can extend legal protection to information the company keeps confidential but which is not technically a trade secret. Fourth, confidentiality agreements can serve to vest in the company all rights in information developed by the employee himself and which an employee might have the right to use for his own purposes absent such an agreement.[1]

Finally, the possession of a signed confidentiality agreement makes injunctive relief against a former employee more likely.

---

[1] T. J. Walsh and R. J. Healey, *Protecting Your Business against Espionage* (New York: AMACOM, 1973).

Courts are understandably reluctant to enjoin an employee from holding a job. But where the employee has signed a confidentiality agreement acknowledging that irreparable injury may result from a breach of his agreement and therefore that an injunction may be entered against him for such a violation (a common provision in confidentiality agreements), a few judges have expressed a greater willingness to enter injunctive relief.

Preliminary Considerations

A confidentiality agreement is coercive by its very nature. It takes away rights in information which the employee would otherwise retain. It also prescribes the penalties for noncompliance with the agreement, and—the final indignity—it requires the employee to stipulate to these penalties. Not only *that*, but the employee doesn't even get anything in return. Most of the time these agreements are tendered to the employee once he has reported for work, and his acquiescence is *not* a bargained-for condition of employment. Thus, both the contents of the typical confidentiality agreement and the manner in which the employee is compelled to accede to its terms seem destined to arouse resentment. But just as a democracy requires the consent of the governed, so does the effective enforcement of a proprietary-information policy require the cooperation of those subject to its directives. Accordingly, if a company wishes to impose on its employees the strictures of an effective confidentiality agreement, it should first enlist their support and persuade them that such restraints will in the long run redound to their own benefit.

This effort can best be initiated by setting forth the company's information-protection policy, and the necessity for the employee restraints, in the letter tendering or confirming an offer of employment. The firm's employee confidentiality agreement should also accompany the offer of employment.

This procedure will accomplish a number of objectives. First, it will inform the prospective employee that entering into the company's confidentiality agreement is bargained for, not imposed. The prospect knows that he has the option of refusing to sign the agreement and rejecting the offer of employment in favor of other opportunities. Second, the applicant is given to understand, right from the inception of the employment relationship, that the company is serious about protecting its investment in research and development. Third, the prospective employee's support in protecting the company's information assets is solicited at the same time the employee may be negotiating over such terms as bonuses and stock options, which are predicated in part upon the preservation and enhancement of company trade secrets. And fourth, the employee is informed what is required of him *before* he has terminated his existing employment and has no choice but to agree.

There are other equally compelling reasons for dealing with the confidentiality agreement before employment actually begins. In several reported cases, confidentiality agreements went unexecuted because someone forgot to deal with the matter when the employee reported for work. Even key personnel sometimes serve several years without being requested to sign a confidentiality agreement because no one was aware that the agreement hadn't been signed when they were hired. This problem can prove difficult to fix in midstream. Some jurisdictions will not enforce restrictive covenants like nondisclosure agreements entered into during the course of employment where there was no independent consideration for them (i.e., the employee received nothing in return). In these states, the employee would have to receive something back, such as a promotion, an increase in salary, etc. for the agreement to be effective. The best way to deal with this issue is to avoid it altogether by having all the formalities of employment agreed on prior to the commencement of employment.

Each company should incorporate into its offer letter language which achieves the aforementioned goals. Sample language is included below for illustration only. It should not simply be copied. Each company should employ its own style and set forth in the offer letter those facts relating to the development of proprietary information and its maintenance which are peculiar to the firm's own experience. Otherwise, the letter will ring false, and will not have the intended effect of impressing on each employee how serious the company is about protecting its proprietary information from disclosure.

> As you may be aware, Computer Industries, Inc., is an industry leader in the mainframe computer market. This market leadership is substantially attributable to the proprietary information which the company has developed over the years, which affords all of us enhanced employment opportunities and is a primary source of increased pay and benefits for each employee of the Company. To acquire its proprietary information and to use it to commercial advantage, we have spent millions of dollars each year in research and product development, on product improvements, and on the enhancement of marketing methods. The pool of proprietary in-

formation the Company has developed has enabled it to conduct its business with considerable success, and helps guarantee the continued success of the Company in the future; but this potential exists only so long as this information remains secret and confidential. Obviously, once it is known by others, any competitive advantage attributable to the Company's proprietary information disappears. This harms both the Company and its employees, whose well-being is inextricably linked to the Company's own success. Obviously, therefore, all of the Company's employees have a common interest in and responsibility for assuring that our Company's proprietary information is not disclosed to or used by others.

To maintain Computer Industries' success and growth, it is extremely important that the Company's proprietary information be protected. In order to provide this protection, the Company requests that each employee sign the enclosed Employee Confidentiality Agreement. This Agreement sets forth the duties and obligations of the Company's employees with respect to the protection of the Company's proprietary information. Your signature will assure that the Company and yourself have a common understanding as to your responsibilities in the effort to protect the confidential information of the Company. Please read the enclosed Agreement carefully and satisfy yourself that you understand its contents fully. The Company will be happy to explain any provision that is unclear to you. Then please sign and date the Agreement and return it to Mr. Smith of our personnel department.

Remember, this is only an exemplar. It will not serve all people or all purposes. Some managers may find it too long, others too conciliatory. But however it is worded, keep in mind that its purpose is not merely to extract a signature, but also to enlist the support of the prospective employee for the company's proprietary information protection policy.

If, after having made these efforts to enlist the employee's cooperation, he refuses to sign, the company assumes a real risk if it employs him anyway. His refusal to sign and his subsequent employment may be taken as either an acknowledgment that no duty of confidentiality arises as to the particular employee, or as a lapse of security undermining the claim that any information he had access to was in fact kept secret. Also, the employee's motive for refusing to sign should be inquired into, for the employee may have future plans which are inconsistent with the company's well-being.

What to Put in the Agreement

Now let's consider the principal provisions of the agreement.

Consideration. The consideration for the employee's agreement—i.e., what the employee is receiving in return—should be stated clearly. This will prevent the employee from later arguing lack of consideration for the agreement. Here is a sample consideration clause:

> The undersigned acknowledges that during his employment he may receive, or gain access to, the proprietary information of the Company, and in consideration for his employment, terminable at will, as a system's engineer and the receipt of stock options for 1,000 shares of Company stock, the undersigned stipulates and agrees as hereinafter set forth.

A Definition of What Is Proprietary. This provision defines what the signatory agrees to keep confidential and not to disclose. The duty of nondisclosure should expressly survive the employment relationship.

Lawyers are apparently of two minds on the issue of subject matter definition. Most confidentiality agreements contain only general descriptions of categories of information a company considers confidential, such as processes, formulas, software data, and the like, on the technical side, and such items as marketing plans, sales, forecasts, and customer lists on the business end.

A boilerplate identification of confidential subject matter along these lines may be quite adequate. In a number of decisions courts enforced confidentiality agreements against employees even though the specific information claimed to be a trade secret or confidential business information was never specifically identified in them. For example, a confidentiality agreement generally prohibiting disclosure of "any information concerning inventions, processes, or methods concerning the company's business" was held to justify an injunction against the use by a former employee of information gleaned from experiments that did not even result in a commercially viable product!

The rationale given for not requiring more specificity in nondisclosure agreements is that a broad enumeration of categories adequately puts the employee on notice that his work may involve proprietary information. The employee is then under a duty to inquire if he is uncertain as to what is deemed proprietary, and if he does use for his own ends information adjudged to be proprietary to his employer, he has no cause to complain if he is held liable.

But this is not a universal attitude by any means. In the Motorola case referred to earlier, Motorola based its case in part on its confidentiality agreement, which generally prescribed that the employee would maintain in confidence any secret information relating to products, machinery, processes, know-how, specifications, and the like. But the departing Motorola executives had never been advised precisely what Motorola actually considered proprietary, even though it was industry practice to do so. In a scathing critique of Motorola's practices, the judge responded to the claim that proprietary information was taken by pungently observing that "the conclusion is inevitable that Motorola did not *know* what it so considered." Indeed, Motorola's attempted enforcement of its ill-defined confidentiality agreement was perceived to be an act of corporate oppression.

Even if this reaction to indefinite generalities in a nondisclosure agreement were unrepresentative, it should give a manager pause. Obviously, the institution of suit against resigning employees for the sin of misappropriating trade secrets the company had never even identified did not sit well in the *Motorola* decision. It is one of the fundamental tenets of our legal system that a person have fair notice of what is required of him. Intentionally failing to identify precisely what a company considers to be proprietary is to court the unnecessary risk that the confidentiality agreement will be disregarded.

The Motorola decision is by no means unique. In a software trade secret case a programmer had signed a typical confidentiality agreement providing that he would not reveal any information concerning the company's business, including its inventions, shop practices, processes, and methods of manufacturing and merchandising. The Minnesota Supreme Court refused to give an expansive interpretation to the agreement, saying that the programmer was entitled to fair notice of what information he was expected to keep confidential. Indeed, the court interpreted the agreement to cover only "that which an employee knew or should have known was confidential." Because there was no precise definition, delineation, or enumeration of what the company considered confidential, the court held that the programmer had no express notice of what information was to be kept confidential; and since the company had failed to take reasonable precautions to protect its software, the employee was deemed not to have had constructive knowledge of what was considered confidential either. The want of definition in the employee confidentiality agreement effectively nullified the agreement. Decisions in other jurisdictions have reached the same result.

Solving the problem by calling *everything* confidential won't work either. For example, a few years ago, a distributor sued a former employee for allegedly utilizing the company's trade secrets. The employee had signed a confidentiality agreement which provided that every type of information be obtained pertaining to the distributor's existing or contemplated business was a trade secret. Disregarding the terms of the confidentiality agreement and finding in favor of the employee, the judge caustically remarked: "the definition of secrets so as to include information of every kind obtained by the employee is absurd." Besides irritating judges, such all-inclusive claims of confidentiality encompass the general skill and experience all employees obtain on the job and which they cannot be prohibited from using. Thus, such confidentiality clauses are overbroad from the start, and may be ruled void for that reason.

Finally, an overzealous enumeration of confidential items of information has frequently been disregarded by judges who deemed such a provision to intrude on their prerogative to determine whether a claim of trade secrecy or confidentiality was supported by the evidence. A number of cases are in accord with one court's ruling that it was not bound by the enumeration of confidential subject matter in a confidentiality agreement because: "[s]uch an agreement cannot make secret that which is not secret, and it remains for the court to determine whether an alleged trade secret is in fact such." Admittedly, there is not unanimity on this issue. In a few instances an employee acknowledgment that certain information was secret was determined to be a binding admission on him. But as the use of confidentiality clauses grows, courts are likely to become more discerning in their scrutiny of them, and less likely to forfeit their discretion to determine the issue of secrecy for themselves.

So to be safe, a company should carefully assess what information in its possession really *is* a trade secret and what information it really would be deleterious to disclose. Though it may be impractical to identify each and every item of proprietary material, the specific nature of the material claimed to be secret can readily be identified. Thus, instead of generally claiming, for example, that "software" is regarded by the company as confidential, it would be wiser to also designate *which* categories of software are so regarded by the company. Instead of just "processes," the nature of the processes deemed proprietary should be identified. The same goes for "devices," "methods," and all the other enumerated categories of information so often listed in confidentiality agreements.

Of course, this imposes a substantial administrative burden on the company, which will have to inventory its information as well as its goods. Moreover, as new processes, inventions, and so forth are developed, the identification of proprietary items will have to be constantly revised. But this is all as it should be. A trade secret claim is a serious matter for an employee. Such lawsuits should not be brought based on amorphous perceptions of confidentiality, and trade secrets should not be defined by reference to what a given employee knew when he left. The decision as to what is considered proprietary needs to be made in an organized, systematic fashion prior to the time that litigation with an employee is ever contemplated. Although the inclusion of nonconfidential information within the coverage of an employee confidentiality agreement may not invalidate the agreement, it could make a judge skeptical about a company's good faith in making its proprietary information claims. It must always be kept in mind that in trade secret litigation judges and jurors are often operating in totally unfamiliar territory, and adverse impressions can fatally infect the proceedings. Particularly where a large company with substantial financial resources is proceeding against a former employee, it must both be, and appear to be, scrupulously fair in its dealings with him. The place to start is with a meticulously drawn employee confidentiality agreement that is not overinclusive. Accordingly, the agreement should specifically exclude from its operation any information known in the trade, as well as information that later becomes known. In addition, there should be an exclusion for the general knowledge and skill obtained by the employee during the course of his employment, and information already in his possession. And finally, information in the public domain should, of course, be excepted.

Although the confidentiality agreement should not be overbroad, it should also not be underinclusive either. The agreement should extend to the proprietary information of third parties which has been entrusted to the company. Company employees frequently have access to technology licensed to the company under a contract requiring the licensee to protect the licensed technology from disclosure or use in the same manner as the licensee protects its own proprietary information. And such an obligation aside, the company that has licensed expensive technology has an interest in keeping secret that which it paid for. The scope of the employee confidentiality agreement should therefore be defined so as to include the trade secrets and proprietary information of third parties in the company's possession.

Finally, if it is the company's intention (as it usually will be) to prevent its employees from utilizing proprietary information that they themselves have developed, the confidentiality agreement should expressly say so. As was mentioned earlier (see Chapter 4), if the confidentiality agreement does not cover proprietary information created by an employee, the employee may be accorded the right to use it in the service of a competitor.

Disclaimer of Proprietary Information of Former Employer. It is incumbent on a company, for economic reasons, to do everything possible to avoid legal exposure by avoiding inadvertent access to the proprietary information of other companies. Accordingly, the employee should be required to acknowledge that he has not taken anyone else's proprietary information for use in his new employment. Here is an examplar:

> The undersigned represents that he does not have in his possession any written materials embodying information known or claimed to be the proprietary or confidential information of any other person, and further represents that he has not removed any written material from the premises of a former employer without the written consent of that employer. The undersigned further represents that to his knowledge his employment with the Company will not require him to use or disclose any proprietary or confidential information of any former employer.

Such an effort is not just for show; a company's good faith admonition to a new employee to refrain from bringing proprietary information with him will usually absolve the company from liability for conspiring with the employee to misappropriate trade secrets.

Return of Written Materials. A key employee may be able to inflict considerable damage on a company by utilizing trade secrets or other forms of confidential information that he carried away in his memory. But by far the greatest competitive threat to a company is the misappropriation of information in tangible form. This is attributable both to the limitations of human memory and to the fact the physical misappropriation provides access to volumes of information generated by countless others. Therefore, every nondisclosure agreement should contain a covenant by the employee not to remove any physical embodiments of confidential information from the company premises without authorization, to return all such embodiments of information upon the termination of employment, and to certify in writing that this been done. Each company should specifically enumerate what forms its proprietary information might take. Here is a sample provision:

> The undersigned agrees that he will not remove Proprietary Information in any form from Company premises without prior authorization. The undersigned acknowledges that any and all correspondence, documentation, blueprints, drawings, models, notes, memoranda, notebooks, program listings, and reports he has obtained during the course of his employment constitutes the property of the Company, and the undersigned agrees that he will return all such material, and all copies thereof, to the Company upon the termination of his employment or as requested by the Company, and further agrees to certify in writing when he has done so.

A provision of this sort constitutes an employee's acknowledgment that physical forms of information belong to the company whether or not the information inhering in them is confidential. If it can later be shown that the employee, in violation of this provision, *did* remove documentation, source listings, or the like from the company, the natural inclination of a judge or jury hearing a subsequent trade secret dispute will be suspicion that the information taken *was* proprietary, on the reasoning that there would be no reason to violate one's promise not to remove such written materials unless it did contain valuable information. Moreover, there is inevitably going to be skepticism as to the employee's entire testimony; there will be doubt as to whether someone who violates his employment agreement in one regard by taking written materials can be believed when he asserts that he did not also violate it in another regard by misappropriating the company's trade secrets.

Establishment of a Confidential Relationship. There are a number of relationships for which it is assumed as a matter of law that disclosures of proprietary information will be held in confidence. The employer-employee relationship is usually assumed to be one of them. The law therefore requires employees to maintain their company's proprietary information in confidence, and not to use it themselves or disclose it to another. Accordingly, there is little need for a contract clause establishing the confidential nature of the employer-employee relationship. However, several legal decisions have carved out exceptions for various low-level, nonsupervisory positions. In cases against salesmen, maintenance personnel, and hourly wage earners, some courts have refused to infer a duty of nondisclosure. Under these decisions, such workers would be free to disclose or use any company information to which they have had access, unless they have specifically promised to hold certain information in confidence or the circumstances were such that they should have been aware that such information had been disclosed to them upon an understanding that they would hold it in confidence. A properly drawn confidentiality agreement will take care of the problem. The pertinent clause might go as follows:

> The undersigned agrees that both during and after his employment he will hold the proprietary information of the Company in trust and confidence and will not use or disclose it, or any embodiment thereof, except as may be necessary in the performance of his duties as an employee of the Company and on behalf of the Company.

Moonlighting. Even the most loyal employee would find it hard to segregate what he has learned during his employment from the knowledge he utilizes in a part-time job. There is also the inevitable temptation to fudge a little where the possession of company proprietary information enables the employee to receive a premium for his services. It is therefore advisable to prohibit or circumscribe part-time employment for employees who are privy to company trade secrets. Here is a representative clause:

> The undersigned agrees that while he is employed by the Company, he will not, without the Company's prior written consent, engage in employment which is directly or indirectly related to any line of business in which the Company is now or may hereafter become engaged.

Permission to Contact Subsequent Employer. Suppose a key employee in possession of a company's most critical trade secrets were to resign abruptly, resurfacing a few days later in the employ of a competitor. Suppose further that in anticipation of a legal dispute, he wrote a letter to his former employer expressing his intention not to disclose the company's proprietary information and warning that threats of legal action made against his new employer could result in his loss of employment, for which his former company would be held responsible. The company now has a real dilemma: If its competitor is not given notice of the nature of the trade secret claims and makes some substantial investment to exploit the trade secret information without knowledge that it has received another's trade secrets, it may have no liability to the originator of the trade secrets. On the other hand, if the company does succeed in preventing its trade secrets from being used and the former employee is terminated, it faces the possibility of an unpleasant lawsuit by the employee.

The best way out of this predicament is to avoid it from the outset. The employee confidentiality agreement should confer permission upon the employer to contact a subsequent employer for the purpose of notifying him of the terms of the employment agreement (which will include both an enumeration of the company's trade secrets and the employee's promise not to disclose them). Here is a typical provision to effectuate that objective:

> The undersigned agrees that the Company may inform any person or entity subsequently employing him, or evidencing an intention to employ him, of the nature of the information it asserts to be proprietary, and may inform said person or entity of the existence of this Agreement and the terms hereof, and provide to said person or entity a copy of this Agreement.

Restrictive Covenants.   Noncompetition agreements, whereby an employee agrees not to work for a competitor for a specific period of time after leaving his employment, are often included along with confidentiality agreements. Noncompetition clauses are extremely disfavored by the courts because they severely constrict an employee's opportunities to make a living and because they result in the suppression of competition. The Minnesota Supreme Court, for example, was moved to declare a restrictive covenant "a form of industrial peonage without redeeming virtue in the American enterprise system." Indeed, several states have passed statutes making such clauses illegal. Even in a state in which noncompetition agreements are not illegal, courts scrutinize them closely for "reasonableness."

Courts have advanced any number of reasons for invalidating noncompetition covenants:

1. Where the consideration for the covenant is inadequate or nonexistent.
2. Where the covenant does not advance a legitimate business interest, such as the protection of confidential information or customer relationships.
3. Where the burden inflicted on the employee or the adverse impact to the public is disproportionate to the benefit conferred on the employer.
4. Where the nature of the restricted activity is vaguely worded.
5. Where the employer seeking to enforce a noncompetition covenant has not dealt with its employee in good faith.

6. Where the geographic or temporal scope of the noncompeti-
    tion covenant is too broad.

There are a variety of less onerous restrictions on competitive
employment which are coming to be used in response to judicial
hostility to outright prohibitions against competitive employment. For example, covenants not to solicit a former employer's
customers (the confidential identities of which the employee has
learned in the course of his employment) for a specified period
of time have routinely been enforced, even in states prohibiting
noncompetition agreements, so long as the nonsolicitation period is reasonably related to the amount of time that would be
required to determine customer identities independently. Such a
clause is far less restrictive in its impact than a noncompetition
agreement; indeed, it does not prohibit competitive employment
per se at all.

Narrowly delineated "activity" proscriptions, such as a prohibition on customer solicitation, are likely to be used more frequently in the future. As employment in the knowledge industries becomes more and more specialized, the economic justification for an outright ban on employment with every other company in the industry disappears. As the Wisconsin Supreme
Court noted in a customer solicitation case, in simpler times distinguishing between "competition" on the one hand and the activities conducted on behalf of a competitor on the other would
have been nonsense, since "a trade was a trade, set apart by separate guilds...and there was no ambiguity in a promise not to
'exercise the trade of a baker' or 'enter into competition.'" What
mattered in days of yore was not *what* was proscribed (that was
understood) but *where* the prohibition on competition would be
enforceable. The common-law courts required that noncompetition agreements be circumscribed as to time and geographic
scope, but a specific activity prohibition would have been redun-
dant. However, in a world where goods and services can move
across the country or around the world in a few seconds or a few
hours, it is often the geographic restraint that becomes meaningless. In the future, specific activity restraints will likely stand a
better chance of being upheld than will outright prohibitions on
employment with a competitor.

Liquidated damage provisions have also been utilized by some
companies to moderate the effect of a blanket prohibition on
competitive employment. These provisions are frequently enforced, despite sometimes draconian terms. For example, in one
case the court enforced a $500-per-day liquidated damage provi-

sion. Other forms of liquidated damage provisions that have been used include a lump sum payment upon competitive employment, payment of a specified amount per customer solicited, and a requirement that profit-sharing benefits be repaid upon competitive employment. However, such provisions tend not to be enforced in states which prohibit noncompetition agreements, on the rationale that a penalty imposed upon competitive employment is little better than an absolute prohibition.

Another popular device used by many companies has been an employee's forfeiture of various types of benefits if he becomes employed by a competitor. For example, a number of cases have involved clauses cutting off pension benefits if a former employee goes to work for a competitor. Similar clauses provide for the termination of profit-sharing benefits. These provisions are enforceable if they meet the requirements of the Employee Retirement Income Security Act (ERISA). Another variant on the same theme is the termination of deferred compensation in the event of competitive employment. Some states will enforce such provisions, while others require them to meet the same standards of reasonableness that noncompetition covenants are required to meet.

One excellent way to have benefit termination clauses upheld is to condition termination of payments *not* upon competitive employment, but simply upon termination of employment. The purpose of such "golden handcuff" provisions is to persuade employees to continue their employment with the company, and to deter them from resigning for *any* reason (not just to join a competitor). This is a manifestly permissible purpose. Moreover, a company may well consider it financially inadvisable to continue to pay deferred compensation or similar benefits to a former employee who is no longer contributing to the welfare of the company. These provisions are likely to be upheld even in jurisdictions which frown on noncompetition covenants.

Restrictions on Scope. As we have seen, in assessing the enforceability of noncompetition agreements courts have generally required noncompetition agreements to be limited in time and geographic extent. A few courts have applied the same restrictions to confidentiality agreements. However, there is a fundamental difference between noncompetition agreements and employee confidentiality agreements. The former absolutely prohibits an employee from working for a competitor for a specified period of time, while the latter merely proscribes the use or disclosure of proprietary company information the employee would not be legally entitled to use anyway. Thus, the former proscribes what the law permits, while the latter interdicts what the law already proscribes. Therefore, the social-policy arguments in opposition to the enforcement of nondisclosure agreements are not nearly so compelling as they are for the enforcement of noncompetition agreements.

Regrettably, a few courts have held nondisclosure agreements invalid because they were unlimited as to time. But if the nondisclosure covenant applies only so long as the information covered by the covenant remains confidential, such a requirement is illogical. Proprietary information *should* be protectable indefinitely, until it is no longer secret.

Limitations on the geographic scope of nondisclosure agreements also make little sense. In the context of noncompetition agreements, geographic limitations are of critical importance. A former employer usually has no legitimate interest in prohibiting a former employee from similar employment outside the area served by the former employer. But information does not honor artificial boundaries. The effects of trade secret misappropriation will be equally severe regardless of where the wrongful use or disclosure occurs. Indeed, a geographically unlimited *nondisclosure* provision will normally be less burdensome to an employee than a geographically circumscribed noncompetition agreement. For example, in the customer list context a prohibition against using a former employer's confidential customer list to solicit clients is considerably less onerous than an absolute prohibition on employment in the former employer's market area—i.e., the area where the former employee usually resides and has most of his business and social contacts.

Other Provisions.   There are a number of other clauses customarily included in the agreement which do not specifically relate to common law rights in information, but which pertain, rather, to copyright and contract issues. A discussion of these provisions is beyond the scope of this book.

The Patent and Invention Assignment Agreement

Usually the confidentiality agreement and the patent and invention assignment agreement are contained in the same document. The purpose of the patent and invention assignment agreement is to reorder the respective rights of employee and employer that would be operable in the absence of such an agreement. In the absence of an express agreement to the contrary, the law assumes that an employee is entitled to inventions he has developed, except that if he is hired for the express purpose of invention and development, the product of his work will belong to the employer. However, if an employee uses the resources and facilities of his employer in the development of an invention, the employer has a license-free right to utilize such an invention.

The patent and invention assignment agreement changes all that. Most such agreements vest all rights in inventions and discoveries in the employer. Such an agreement can be subdivided into three subject matter areas: (1) a promise to disclose all inventions and discoveries; (2) an agreement to assign all inventions and discoveries; and (3) a reservation of rights in all inventions and discoveries previously made by the employee. Each of these subparts will be considered in turn.

The Promise to Disclose All Discoveries

The purpose of the first clause of the patent and invention assignment agreement is to define the subject matter of the agreement. In order to discuss this provision intelligently, let us first consider a typical provision:

> The undersigned agrees that he will disclose to the Company all inventions, improvements, software, processes, ideas, and innovations (hereinafter referred to, for convenience only, as "Discoveries"), made or conceived by him, whether or not patentable or copyrightable, either solely or in concert with others, and whether or not made or conceived during working hours, during the period of his employment, which (a) relate to the existing or contemplated business or research activities of the Company; (b) result from the use of the Company's proprietary information, facilities, or resources; or (c) arise out of or result from work performed for the Company. [In appropriate circumstances, the provision should also contain an acknowledgment by the employee that he has been employed to engage in R&D.] The undersigned further agrees to keep full and complete records concerning the development of discoveries as above defined and to tender such records to the company upon request.

This clause implicates a number of issues that have arisen in litigation involving patent and invention assignment agreements. Judges tend to construe these agreements against the employer because they are drafted by the employer and the employer has superior bargaining power. So it is important that the agreement *expressly* apply to discoveries and inventions whether or not they are patentable or can be copyrighted; otherwise, the clause may be construed to apply only to patentable or copyrightable inventions and works.

The lengths to which courts will go to reach this result is illustrated by an Oklahoma decision. The facts are unique. Lindley, an employee of Amoco, requested permission to develop a computerized well-log analysis system, which would assess prospects for finding oil in certain geological formations. His request was denied because someone else had been assigned the task; but Lindley wrote his own software on his own time. Two years later he disclosed his work to his employer, and was immediately directed to cease work on it and to integrate his works into Amoco's existing system. Lindley continued to develop additional capabilities for his program, finally left the company (undoubtedly in frustration), and subsequently joined a competitor. Amoco then demanded all rights to the program under a patent assignment clause in a contract Lindley had signed whereby he agreed to disclose and assign to Amoco all inventions and discoveries capable of use in the company's business. Obviously offended by Amoco's shoddy treatment of its employee, the court looked for a way to avoid enforcing the assignment, and found one. Discovering in Lindley's employment agreement a clause relating to the preparation and filing of patent applications, the court therefore concluded that the assignment clause was only intended to cover *patentable* inventions. Since (at the time) computer programs were assumed not to be patentable, the court ruled that the assignment clause therefore did not apply to Lindley's computer program. This case illustrates how important it is that the assignment agreement explicitly apply to both patentable and nonpatentable discoveries.

A limitation to discoveries relating to the business of or relating to work performed for the company contained in the sample provision is not only just and reasonable, but is required in some places by statute. Moreover, what business justification is there for demanding the rights to an innovative new toy designed by an aerospace engineer in his spare time? Only where the employee has used the facilities or trade secrets of the company, or where the invention or discovery relates to the company's business or research or evolves from the ordinary course of the employee's activities, is there a commercial rationale for demanding the assignment of an employee's discoveries. Most companies don't really want any other rights anyway, and to require the employee to surrender the products of his tinkering will certainly cause a good deal of resentment among the company's most creative individuals.

The most substantial issue presented by the sample provision is the extent to which a company may require the "assignment" of intangible concepts and ideas. Such a clause obviously has some anticompetitive potential, since a subsequent development by a former employee in a competitor's employ could provoke the contention that the development was really based on an idea or concept already assigned.

The ability of a company to suppress new product ideas by resort to an assignment clause is illustrated by a New Jersey action in which two men hired by a tennis ball machine manufacturer had signed invention assignment agreements. They conceived of an idea for a smaller, improved machine and, after receiving little support for the idea from the chairman of the board, left the company and implemented their idea themselves. In finding that the new design belonged to their former employer, the court relied in part on the assignment agreements they had signed.

However, it would not be overstating the case to say that idea assignment clauses are not popular with the courts, and judges have been quite inventive in construing them away. For example, if a discovery assignment provision does not expressly apply to intangible ideas, the agreement certainly will not be construed to apply to intangible forms of information by implication. In one case, for example, an employee had signed an agreement providing for the assignment of all "inventions or improvements" made by him during his employment, and requiring him to disclose all such inventions or improvements. During the course of his employment, the employee, who was director of research, conceived of an idea for a ball valve that would control fluid flow in two directions instead of just one. Instead of disclosing his idea to his employer, he withheld it, set up his own company, and then reduced his idea to design and practice. Despite the somewhat questionable ethics of the employee's conduct, the court ruled that the concept of "invention" quite clearly contemplated some form of reduction to practice or tangible form so that the employee could not be held liable for violating the invention assignment clause.

Even language dictating the assignment of discoveries and inventions *conceived* of during employment may not remedy the problem. In a case involving precisely that language, an employee of a road construction equipment company resigned, and, within a matter of a few days, had developed sketches for an improved piece of equipment, which was ultimately manufactured. But the trial judge characterized these sketches as "merely rough ideas of alternatives," and declined the company's invitation to infer from the proximity in time between the employee's resignation and the sketches that the designs embodied in the sketches were in fact discoveries or inventions developed during the period of employment. The judge concluded that such an assignment agreement "does not give an employer a mortgage on all thoughts occurring to the employee, but is limited to those ideas which . . . can in fact be deemed an improvement, discovery, or invention and are sufficiently concrete to be considered a development or conception." Another court construed a similar clause to apply only to "unique ideas" and "particularized proposals," so that even product proposals actually submitted by employees to their employer did not vest in the company all rights in the product idea if the proposals were "general" and contained no new ideas.

There are two perspectives on the practice of importing a concreteness and particularity requirement into invention assignment clauses. On one hand, it disposes of the need for the courts to serve as "thought police," investigating whether or not an employee had a given idea during the course of his prior employment; there is something vaguely Orwellian about making thoughts and ideas the object of judicial scrutiny. On the other hand, making concreteness a prerequisite to the assignment of rights in an invention or discovery does permit an employee who has agreed to assign to his employer inventions and assignments conceived of during employment to originate a commercially feasible idea and then resign in order to exploit it himself and deprive his employer of its benefits.

Some companies have tried to forestall such conduct by requiring the assignment of inventions and discoveries developed not only during the course of employment but for some period of time thereafter. This means that an employee who subsequently went to work for a competitor would have to disclose to his former employer all discoveries and inventions made in the service of his new employer. Courts have limited the effect of such clauses only to subject matter an employee worked on or knew about during his previous tenure, but even with that limitation such postemployment restraints would so seriously reduce a person's employment opportunities during the period of the restraint that they have frequently been held contrary to public policy and therefore void. For example, in one case a company tried to enforce against former employees an assignment agreement requiring the disclosure of inventions and discoveries during the period of their employment and for a period of five years thereafter insofar as they related to the business of the company. The judge had little difficulty in ruling that this contractual provision unreasonably restricted the employees' ability to earn a living, that it violated the public policy of encouraging employees to improve themselves, and that it unreasonably frustrated competition. Although a few courts have allowed post-employment assignment provisions, these clauses are most likely to be enforced where limited to the assignment of discoveries and inventions based on the former employer's trade secrets or confidential information.

The Assignment Clause

The invention and discovery assignment clause is fairly straightforward. Its primary purpose is to formally transfer rights in inventions and discoveries to the company and to assure the employee's cooperation in achieving that goal. A typical provision might read as follows:

> The undersigned hereby assigns to the Company his entire right, title, and interest in and to all discoveries as above defined, which he may develop or originate alone or with others, and the undersigned agrees that all such discoveries and inventions shall be the exclusive property of the Company, and are reserved for the exclusive use and benefit of the Company. The undersigned further agrees to assist the Company in obtaining and enforcing patents, copyrights, and/or any other statutory or common-law protection available as to such discovery or invention whether under foreign or domestic law. The undersigned further agrees to execute all documents deemed necessary or advisable by the Company for use in applying for or obtaining patents, copyrights, or any other statutory or common-law protection for such discoveries and inventions, and for enforcing same. The undersigned acknowledges that his obligations under this Paragraph shall continue beyond the termination of his employment, but that after such termination the Company will compensate him at a reasonable rate for time actually spent at the Company's request for such assistance.

The effect of such a clause is to completely divest the employee of any rights in or to any developments created by him during the course of his employment. If the employee expects to be compensated for discoveries that confer a substantial benefit on his employer, this needs to be expressly embodied in the discovery assignment agreement itself. Most such agreements will contain what is called an integration clause, reciting that there are no other agreements pertaining to the same subject matter. So if someone has promised additional compensation for patents or other discoveries that confer an unusual benefit on the company, the assignment clause should reflect that agreement; otherwise, it may not count.

The Employee Disclaimer

Because the discovery assignment clause applies only to discoveries and inventions developed during the course of employment, there should be some way to distinguish those discoveries and inventions from others the employee may have made earlier or is in the process of making. An employee disclaimer clause will meet this objective. Here is an example:

> The undersigned represents that he has identified on Exhibit A a complete list of all discoveries and inventions which he has made or conceived of prior to the commencement of his employment with the Company, and which are not to be covered by the terms of this Agreement. (If there are no such discoveries designated, the undersigned acknowledges that he has neither made nor conceived of any such discoveries or inventions as of the time of signing this Agreement.)

Giving the employee the initiative to define his prior discoveries himself has a couple of advantages. First, the employee is permitted to define the scope of the exclusion himself. Second, since it is in the employee's interest to make the exclusion as broad as possible, if there are going to be problems they can be identified *before* the employee commences work. For obvious reasons, the company cannot permit the employee to exclude from the operation of the agreement the company's principal trade secrets; the exclusions need to be sufficiently well defined to distinguish the employee's prior discoveries from company proprietary information.

One note here for employees. Devote serious thought to the exclusion clause. Anything not excluded will be assigned to the employer. Not only might this impair rights in inventions the employee might someday wish to exploit on his own, but it could also have an impact on his subsequent employment opportunities.

The discovery exclusion provision raises an associated issue. As was discussed earlier (see Chapter 4) a principal issue in trade secret disputes between employees and their former employers is whether the information in dispute represents the secrets of the employer or the knowledge and experience of the employee. The employee can therefore utilize the occasion of the confidentiality agreement discussions to define the scope of his prior knowledge and expertise. Obviously, some judgment is needed here; it would be ridiculous to try to set forth everything one has learned in the course of prior education and employment. But the constituents of the employee's knowledge and experience which may be of commercial significance should be identified by category. Such a practice should foreclose subsequent claims that information previously known to the employee is proprietary to the company.

The issues implicated in confidentiality and discovery assignment agreements are absolutely central to the distribution of rights in information between employer and employee. Obviously, utilizing all the clauses set forth in this chapter will result in an agreement that is a fairly daunting document, and there are several provisions which have not even been discussed. Many companies disfavor long employee agreements. But one would be hard-pressed to identify any provision set forth above which could safely be disposed of. It is better to tolerate a complicated legal document than to risk jeopardizing rights in proprietary information that may have cost millions of dollars to develop.

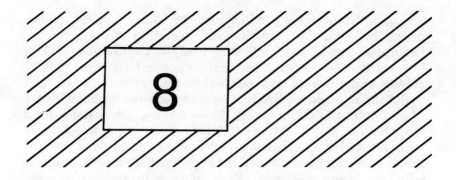

The Sweet Sorrow of Parting
The Severance of the Employment Relationship

In the course of human affairs, as Shakespeare noted, when troubles arrive they come not singly but in battalions. When an employee's departure precipitates a trade secret lawsuit by his former employer, he will also usually be accused of various breaches of his fiduciary obligations for such conduct as preparing to compete while still employed or for solicitation of other employees or customers. We will consider each in turn.

Preparing to Compete

In a world of unlimited resources and boundless opportunity, peopled with persons of a saintly disposition, an employee who desired to go into business for himself would immediately resign. He would speak to no one beforehand—least of all his colleagues and customers of the company. He would then begin to think about what line of business he was interested in pursuing and upon hitting on a product idea, he would then commence preparations for the formation and operation of his company. Perhaps a year later, he might be ready to begin operations. A few courts have even dictated that corporate fiduciaries such as officers and directors must so conduct themselves.

But in the world we live in, few entrepreneurs have the luxury of proceeding in this manner. While making preparations for a new venture, most budding capitalists have to work to eat. They will already have formulated a specific notion of what product line they wish to pursue, and those product ideas will undoubtedly have been suggested by their own employment experience. Indeed, unless the employee is independently wealthy, his only opportunity to start a business will be in a line of activity closely related to his prior employment. No right-thinking venture capitalist or banker will commit funds to an inexperienced executive or engineer who has a good idea but not the background to know whether it is commercially feasible or how to execute it. In most cases, the proposed venture will be one which the employee has dedicated a great deal of thought to, fraught as it is with risk for himself and his family. He may have consulted with colleagues, and perhaps enlisted their participation. He may even have had some customer contact. He will usually have engaged in some preparatory activities, perhaps at the expense of his employment duties. This is the real-life context in which new companies are formed, and each aspect has legal implications that both employer and employee should be aware of.

The nature of an employee's obligation to inform his employer of his prospective plans to compete has gradually changed. Originally most legal decisions postulated an employee's legal duty to fully and completely disclose both his intention to form a competing venture and the details of his preparations. But in these cases the employee's concealment of his plans had provided the opportunity to commit other acts of treacherous misconduct. For example, in one case the employee defendants, during the period of concealment of their plans, had (1) used their employer's machine drawings to develop their own equipment; (2) used their employer's patterns to fabricate their own castings; (3) induced other employees to resign and go to work for a machine shop that was constructing their machinery; (4) used their employer's accounting personnel to perform services for themselves; and (5)—and perhaps most galling—lavishly entertained customers and conferred expensive gifts upon them at their employer's expense immediately prior to terminating their employment.

This is admittedly an extreme illustration. Often an employee will conceal his competitive plans simply to test the market or curry favor with his employer's existing customers. A more prosaic example of concealment to procure a competitive advantage concerned several employees of a data processing company who decided to form a rival company, but continued to work on a project for a government agency client without disclosing their plans—thereby enabling them to assess the needs of the client and solidify their relationships with agency personnel. After they terminated their employment, their new company submitted to the client a bid for a continuation of the project they had been working on in their former company's employ. Recognizing that on account of the concealment of their plans the employees had deprived their employer of the opportunity to consolidate its own bargaining position by using other employees on the project, the court enjoined the submission of a bid by the employees' new company.

Obviously, concealing plans to compete in order to obtain an unfair advantage is conduct which need not be condoned. But just as obviously, a per se rule that employees cannot make preparations to compete without fully informing their present employer of their plans should not be encouraged. As the Maryland Supreme Court observed, a rule requiring employees to disclose their plans to compete in all instances would make the right to plan a new venture "practically meaningless." Indeed, the most likely result of such a revelation would be a swift invitation to the door. And even a less decisive response by the employer could leave the atmosphere so poisoned as to make it necessary for the employee to terminate his employment for the good of all. A rule requiring employees to disclose their intentions to enter the service of a rival would also be difficult to administer because it would be hard to specify precisely when a casual interest in another opportunity coalesced into an active intention to compete. Finally, there seems to be no policy reason why an employee should be forced to disclose his future plans and risk immediate unemployment when his preparations are in no way injurious to his present employer's immediate interests.

This is indeed the tenor of more recent decisions. Most courts have allowed employees to secretly make preparations to compete so long as they do not take advantage of the circumstances to do something their employer could have protected against had it known of their plans. What this means in practice is that employees may conduct such activities as incorporating a new business entity, seek financing or a bank loan, purchase land, lease facilities and buy equipment, and hire employees (except perhaps their colleagues; more on this later). Generally speaking, permissible preparations to compete include anything that would enable the new enterprise to commence operations as soon as the employee terminates his employment.

But having said that, it should also be noted that if an employee does not disclose his plans, he must exercise extreme restraint. The employee who is working for a company and yet making preparations to compete with it in the future has created for himself a potential conflict of interest he must bend over backward to avoid. In the eyes of the law, an employee has no right to do anything contrary to his employer's interests so long as he continues to accept his paycheck. Dissatisfied employees have a natural and understandable inclination to feel that because they are suffering under the yoke of a tyrannical superior, or laboring in a dead-end job beneath their abilities, they are therefore entitled to cut corners in establishing a competing enterprise or joining a competitor. But a judge will not look at the matter from the same perspective; he will see only the pile of cut corners. It is senseless to jeopardize a new enterprise by courting an adverse judgment in a lawsuit or to have one's new employer joined in a lawsuit.

Accordingly, an employee in the process of forming a new venture or joining a rival should steer well clear of the zone of questionable conduct. He should conduct all activities in furtherance of the new venture on his own time. The employee should also refrain from employing his employer's facilities and resources to benefit a rival. Thus, he should avoid using his employer's materials, computer and research facilities, and personnel. Indeed, the employee should even refrain from using his employer's telephone, library, technical reference materials, and the like. Unless he plans to pay for it himself, he should also avoid ordering materials which he may need for a new business opportunity.

Appearances are very important, and such conduct as devoting attention to one's own enterprise at the expense of one's employment duties, failing to give reasonable notice, failing to cooperate with one's replacement, and copying even nonconfidential material has contributed to employees being held liable to their former employers. In fact, one court even made a breach of fiduciary duty by an employee grounds for enjoining the use of non-confidential information acquired in the course of employment. Two employees of a firm that made industrial boiler safety controls formed a competitive venture and began operations while one of them was still employed with the old firm. Finding this conduct to be in obvious breach of the employees' fiduciary obligations, the court then proceeded to enjoin the use of *any* information acquired in their previous employment in competition with their former employer for a period of two years, whether such information constituted a trade secret or not!

Thus, an independent breach of an employee's fiduciary duty resulted in the *de facto* loss of a trade secret claim without the employer even having to prove the existence of a trade secret. Such an outcome is only the most extreme example of the more general truth that disloyal conduct independent of trade secret misappropriation is inevitably going to taint a contemporaneously-asserted trade secret claim.

Soliciting Colleagues

There are two aspects to the problem of employee solicitation: (1) solicitation by the competitor; and (2) solicitation by an employee planning to join the competitor.

Recruitment by a Competitor

A company may hire employees from its competitors (except when they are under contract, which is almost never) at any time, unless its purpose is to destroy the competitor or cripple its ability to compete. This is so, regardless of the effect it may actually have on the competitor. As Judge Learned Hand wrote many years ago: "[i]t has never been thought actionable to take away another's employee, when the defendant wants to use him in his own business, however much the plaintiff may suffer. It is difficult to see how servants could get the full value of their services on any other terms; time creates no prescriptive right in other men's labor." What that means, to descend from the stately to the prosaic, is that "you don't own 'em just because you hire 'em, no matter how long you keep 'em." Too many managers lose sight of that fact, especially after many years of association. The employer-employee relationship is, as a matter of law (and therefore as a matter of fact), strictly a commercial affair. Employees of long standing have as much right as the most transient of workers to join the competition, and rivals have the complementary right to offer them employment.

Only when the solicitation and hiring of a competitor's employees are done for an improper purpose will the law intervene. For example, hiring a competitor's employees to gain access to a rival's proprietary information will certainly result in liability. In one particularly flagrant case, a company located in Philadelphia that wanted to learn how to make telephone cord armor advertised for employees in want ads in Mattoon, Illinois— which just happened to be the town where the only successful manufacturer of telephone cord armor had its plant. From the information conveyed by the new hires, the defendant was able to construct a copy of the plaintiff's manufacturing machinery. The court, not surprisingly, held the company liable for trade secret misappropriation, stating that it knew or should have known that the information conveyed to it by the plaintiff's former employees constituted a disclosure of the cord armor manufacturer's trade secret. And when several employees of Sperry Rand left to found National Semiconductor Corporation, the trial judge concluded that their wholesale recruitment of Sperry employees manifested an intent to misappropriate Sperry's transistor production processes, which these employees were already trained to use.

The propriety of hiring a competitor's employee who had access to trade secrets in his former employment is often judged on appearances. If such an employee is placed in a newly created position with exactly the same responsibilities he had in his previous job, a court might well infer that the new employer was not interested so much in the employee as in the proprietary information he could bring with him. And giving unusually handsome compensation packages has also been cited as evidence of an intention to buy trade secrets and not just an employee. In the celebrated case between Telex Corporation and IBM, Telex offered one former IBM employee a half-million-dollar performance bonus—the largest in the company's history—and hired another former IBM engineer at double his previous salary. The judge looked askance at evidence like that. Even less dramatic increases in compensation have been construed in some cases as evidence of an intention to appropriate a competitor's proprietary information. And performance incentives—which only motivate employees to "borrow" from the proprietary information of their previous employer—are particularly inadvisable if a trade secret dispute can be anticipated.

It is also unlawful to solicit a competitor's employees with the intention of driving the competitor out of business, but just when such an intent arises almost defies definition. For example, whereas in one case hiring away 30 employees from a rival was simply considered vigorous competition, the hiring of 28 employees from a much larger entity was held in another case to have been actuated by an illegal intention to cripple its ability to compete. Although it is difficult to guess when a judge or jury will find the requisite unlawful intent, the one thing that is safe to say is that if there have been any expressed intentions to harm the former employer's business, there is exposure not merely for a breach of fiduciary duty claim, but for a treble-damage antitrust claim as well. In no context can it be more truly said that "loose lips sink ships."

A third aim of recruiting a competitor's employees that some courts regard as improper is solicitation for the purpose of diverting business from the competitor. But the attitude of judges on this matter can differ radically. One federal court decision went so far as to hold solicitation of a few employees of a rack jobber over a one-year period, with the expectation that they would bring customers with them, to be not merely unfair competition, but an *antitrust* violation. The Mississippi Supreme Court on the other hand rejected the contention that there was anything wrong with enticing away most of a competing dental supply company's employees with the same expectation of diverting business. Indeed, the court stated that it was perfectly legitimate for a salesman to sound out his customers before changing employers.

The Recruitment of Colleagues

Courts have dealt fairly leniently with an employee's solicitation of his former colleagues so long as it occurs after he has resigned and accepted employment with another company. Under such circumstances, the solicitation comes under the general rule that any employee employed at will (i.e., for no fixed term) can be solicited and hired by anyone else. Even where the solicitation is conducted by the employee's former supervisor, once the latter has terminated his employment, he is no longer in a position to influence or pressure his subordinates to join him. Of course, there is always the risk that the employer may contend the solicitation really occurred prior to the employee's termination, or was part and parcel of an organized scheme entered into prior to the employee's departure to accomplish some impermissible purpose; such claims, however, have not been notoriously successful where they have been advanced.

But what of the employee who recruits his colleagues and subordinates—i.e., his own employer's employees—while he is still on the company payroll? It is certainly not in the best interests of his employer for such an employee to urge fellow employees to join a competitor and not to report such insurrection to management; therefore, shouldn't it be considered a breach of the employee's fiduciary obligations to engage in such conduct?

On the whole the courts have been unusually tolerant of such conduct. An example from the electronics industry illustrates the point well. An employee of United Aircraft Corporation had recruited a number of his colleagues to join him in a new venture. The court rejected the contention that this collective departure manifested an intent to inflict competitive injury on United Aircraft. The judge acknowledged that some adverse competitive impact on United Aircraft might have been foreseeable (as would occur with *any* new market entrant), but found the plan to form a new company to have been actuated by an intention on the part of the departing employees simply to better themselves and not to inflict injury on their employer. With some logic, the judge asserted that since an outside employer would have been permitted to recruit the employees who left United Aircraft's employ, then certainly those same employees should not be prevented from joining together (i.e., recruiting themselves) in a new enterprise to their mutual benefit. One court even elevated the right to recruit colleagues into a quasi-constitutional right to freedom of association.

As a matter of fact, even the recruitment of almost an entire work force has not resulted in liability in several cases. For example, in one case the division manager of a lubricant manufacturer in the St. Louis area had formed a competitor, resigned, and brought almost all the St. Louis employees with him to his new venture. He was found not to have been in breach of his fiduciary obligations for conducting his recruitment in secrecy, however, because preparations to compete may be made by an employee without disclosing his intentions to his employer. The court acknowledged that an inference of a conspiracy to ruin the former employer could be drawn from the mass exodus of employees. But the court rejected the inference in the absence of any evidence of solicitation of customers, disparagement of the former employer's goods, or an intention to hire away employees for the purpose of acquiring trade secrets.

One decision even legitimated recruitment of a substantial proportion of a dental supply company's local employees by the company's St. Louis general manager while *he was still employed by the company*. The general manager's conduct was characterized as merely informational—i.e., he was supposedly merely informing the other employees of a new opportunity! And the court drew great solace from the fact that the general manager did not tender an offer of employment to anyone who did not request an application.

On the other hand, *less* extreme conduct has been held to be illegal. One Oregon federal court judge found an insurance agent liable for unfair competition simply for recruiting his fellow agents to join him in jumping ship to another company. And employees of a career counseling service who secretly formed a competing venture and solicited employees while they were still on the payroll were slapped with an injunction; it was even held that the solicitation of colleagues *after* their departure was a violation of law.

Despite these differences of opinion as to the practice of colleague recruitment, courts have uniformly disapproved of the practice of using or conveying confidential personnel information about colleagues and subordinates with whom one is still employed in furtherance of their recruitment by a competitor. As was discussed earlier (see pp. 43–44), this has been true not only for detailed personnel data, such as the terms of an employee's compensation, but also for information as imprecise as employee evaluations. The California Supreme Court's opinion in *Bancroft-Whitney Co. v. Glen* provides a good exposition of judges' general views on the subject. In this case a legal publisher, Matthew Bender, carried out a raid on Bancroft-Whitney personnel and enlisted Bancroft-Whitney's president, Glen, in the effort. Glen both participated in the recruitment of his subordinates and provided to Matthew Bender personnel information to enable it to better conduct its recruitment effort. In condemning Glen's provision of personnel information to a competitor, the California Supreme Court wrote:

> It is beyond question that a corporate officer breaches his fiduciary duties when, with the purpose of facilitating the recruiting of the corporation's employees by a competitor, he supplies the competitor with a selective list of the corporation's employees who are, in his judgment, possessed of both ability and the personal characteristics desirable in an employee, together with the salary the corporation is paying the employee and a suggestion as to the salary the competitor should offer in order to be successful in recruitment.

It is obviously difficult to make any sweeping generalizations about these employee-solicitation cases. The most that can be said is that an employee who recruits his colleagues to leave their employment for a new opportunity bears some legal risk, the degree of which depends on the circumstances. But an employee planning to start a new venture or join a competitor and who either wants to keep his managerial or engineering team together or who has other reasons for wanting to solicit his colleagues' participation can, by staying within the bounds of fair and honorable conduct, minimize his legal exposure while still maintaining a reasonably good chance of achieving his recruitment goals.

An excellent example of this proposition is provided by the previously referred to *Motorola* decision, where a number of leading lights in the semiconductor industry left Motorola at approximately the same time to join Fairchild. Fairchild had first contacted one of the departing managers and had conducted discussions with him as to his interest in becoming its chief executive. During the course of these discussions, the manager did not recruit his fellow executives to join him; but he *did* seek the counsel of his colleagues, which any executive should certainly be entitled to do. Quite naturally, some of those executives with whom he conversed indicated an interest in joining his management team if he did accept the position, but the manager declined to discuss employment at Fairchild with any of them, and did no more than provide the telephone number of an executive at Fairchild. The other executives then independently applied for employment with Fairchild and negotiated their own compensation packages. Under such circumstances, the court's finding that there was no illicit conspiracy among the departing employees is not surprising.

A few basic rules of conduct will serve to avoid liability for employee solicitation in most circumstances. First and foremost, an intention to inflict competitive injury on one's existing employer, however vaguely worded and no matter how badly one has been treated, should *never* be expressed in any way at any time. Of course, such an intention should also not be reflected in any writing of any kind, be it a letter, a memorandum, or just the back of an envelope. If it is written down, not only is it evidence, but it is *physical* evidence that a judge or jury can read and reread during deliberations while deciding what is going to be done to you for writing it. The same is true, of course, regarding the expression of any other improper purpose, such as seeking to acquire proprietary information.

It is also a good idea to avoid any possible imputation of conspiratorial motive by not doing anything that could be construed as scheming to the detriment of one's employer. In most cases, for example, there is little need for departing employees to recruit their subordinates or colleagues while still on the company payroll. There may be security in knowing who one's employees are going to be, but such recruitment is best carried out after termination of employment so that the former employer cannot complain to a sympathetic judge that its employees were taking its money with one hand and stabbing the company in the back with the other. And if it is the intention of several employees to join a rival at the same time, at the very least they should make their own economic arrangements independent of each other.

Third, employees should not convey confidential personnel information about their colleagues to anyone. If an employee has accepted a position with another company and the company is interested in knowing what it would take to successfully recruit his colleagues, the company can ask them directly.

Finally, radical increases in salary and benefits should be avoided where a trade secret dispute is anticipated. It is certainly the case that getting good people for a new venture requires attractive compensation packages; but if the possibility of a trade secret claim from another company already exists, hiring its employees is going to exacerbate the situation. And hiring away employees at inflated salary levels is just asking for trouble. If a new enterprise needs to pay a good deal more to attract quality employees, it should hire from companies other than the one threatening a lawsuit. And as was noted earlier, offering performance bonuses when a trade secret dispute is anticipated is just an open invitation to trouble.

These guidelines may seem unduly restrictive, since the majority of cases appear, if not to approve the recruitment of colleagues or the solicitation of groups of a rival's employees, then at least to tolerate such practices. But where there is potential exposure on a trade secret claim as well, excessive caution is warranted. In a close case, the contemporaneous recruitment of employees familiar with their employer's proprietary information, or the well-orchestrated departure of many key employees at the same time, may convince the judge or jury of illicit motive, which will make it much easier to find in the employer's favor on the trade secret claim.

The Solicitation of Clients and Customers

The first question that occurs to an employee contemplating starting a new venture is: "Should I take it?" But as soon as the answer to the first question inclines to the affirmative, the native hue of resolution is sicklied over by the pale cast of thought, and another question immediately rears itself: "What am I going to do for business?" Of course one fertile source of business is constantly fixed before his eyes—his employer's own customers. He may resist the allure of all that business successfully for an extended period of time. But as the day of departure draws near and the insecurity level soars, the temptation to solicit just a *few* company customers may become overpowering. There is a very human tendency to want to reduce the risks of a new venture by investigating the potential for business from existing customers and clients.

These inclinations should be resolutely resisted. With few exceptions, the courts have taken a *very* dim view of an employee soliciting business—even future business—from the customers and clients of his present employer. This is regarded as direct competition with the employer, and some judges describe it in terms more commonly attributed to Judas or Benedict Arnold. Courts take diversions of corporate business seriously because they recognize how very vulnerable a corporation is to depredations from within. As one court wrote: "Because corporate managerial personnel enjoy a high degree of trust and confidence in performing their assigned functions, a potential exists for serious abuse of confidentiality whenever personnel attempt to aggrandize their own economic interests at the expense of the employer." Without question, actively soliciting an employer's existing customers while one is still on the payroll is a breach of fiduciary duty, and in addition to having money damages awarded against him, the employee may be enjoined from doing business with customers so obtained for some period of time.

The reach of the law also extends well beyond an employee's outright solicitation of his employer's customers and clients. In a celebrated New York case, a revolt against the president of an advertising agency resulted in a number of officers and directors of the agency sounding out their accounts to determine the clients' receptivity to their forming a new company or buying out the principal shareholder. That conduct, however, was cited as part of a course of conduct designed to destroy the ad agency and was found to be in breach of fiduciary obligations owed to the employer. Even mere "overtures" by employees to a single company client have been held to constitute wrongful solicitation resulting in an injunction preventing the employee's new enterprise from bidding for that client's business. At times the rule against solicitation has been applied with draconian rigor. In one case, an employee planning to leave did no more than ask for business from three personal friends who were then company customers. This was deemed unlawful solicitation.

There is *one* communication an employee may have with his employer's customers without violating his legal duties to his employer; he may inform customers of the prospective termination of his employment. One false step, however, can mean the entry of an injunction. When, for example, a driver on a dairy route informed many of his customers that he was terminating his employment—perfectly permissible under the law—he also unfortunately added that he would be returning to solicit their business later in the week on his own behalf. The Minnesota Supreme Court deemed the aggregate effect of his communications to his route customers to constitute unfair competition, and held that he should have been enjoined from doing business with those customers until his former employer had had an adequate opportunity to solicit their continued patronage.

Obviously customer contact by an employee in the process of changing employment is a delicate matter. The employee always runs the risk that a customer might construe a simple announcement of a change of employment as a solicitation of business. This can be embarrassing from a business standpoint, for if the customer or client *is* inclined to engage the employee prospectively, the employee is legally obligated to spurn the offer and terminate the discussion. And a misunderstanding on the part of the customer or client can be *legally* embarrassing, since it would be natural for a judge to assume that if the customer thought his business was being solicited, then it *was* being solicited.

There *are* decisions here and there tolerating the acceptance of a few orders by a departing employee who did not actively solicit them or approving the practice of canvassing customers before making a decision to change employers. But an employee should not rely on them. In the area of pretermination customer solicitation, it just does not pay to play brinksmanship with a lawsuit; the odds are badly stacked against the employee. While there is always a possibility of getting away with pretermination customer solicitation, either by not getting caught or by persuading a judge to look the other way, one must seriously question whether the benefit gained is worth the risk of an expensive lawsuit and the imposition of damages or an injunction, especially against a company in its infancy.

There is one other issue that often arises when an employee jumps ship. It is often the case that consummating a business transaction will take months—sometimes years. Can an ex-employee who conducted such negotiations continue these discussions on behalf of a rival?

Although there are a few decisions to the effect that lower-level employees do not owe a fiduciary obligation to their employers and can divert transactions in negotiation to another company, in most jurisdictions business opportunities of which an employee gained knowledge during the course of his employment may not be interfered with if the dealings between company and customer created a legitimate expectation that the company would receive the business. For example, it has been the custom in the construction of water and sewer projects for a municipality to have a preliminary study prepared by an engineering firm, and then to ascertain if federal funding would be available to construct the project; if so, a contract would be let for the preparation of plans. In one Georgia case a civil engineering firm prepared such a study, and then one of its officers, who had secretly formed a competing firm, tried to divert the contract to his own company. Because the officer's former employer was found to have had a reasonable expectancy of getting the contract, the employee was probibited from soliciting the contract for his company. But the expectancy must relate to a *particular* transaction; a course of dealing with one company over many years does not create a legally-recognized expectancy that one will receive any further business.

This is a fair and equitable resolution of the issue. As another judge noted in holding an insurance agent liable for terminating his employment and then diverting to his new company group insurance plans he had been negotiating on behalf of his previous employer: "in a sense he is delivering the proceeds or the fruits of his work for one employer to his new employer." Of course, it may be that a company is just using such an interference with economic relations claim as a pretext to prevent competition by a former employee; but if there is a basis for asserting a legitimate expectancy of receiving certain identifiable contracts, there is no policy reason why a former employee should be allowed to divert these opportunities when he leaves his employment.

The Termination Minuet

A key employee's announcement of his intention to join a competitive entity (a competitor or his own firm) commences a sensitive period for both the existing and the prospective employer. It is at this time that the existing employer will seek to widen the scope of the information to be protected against disclosure to the prospective employer, and the prospective employer needs to be alert to prevent its new employee from compromising its own competitive position.

The sophisticated company will have initiated defensive measures long before the employee was ever offered employment. A company with a particularized need for an employee in an area of work that customarily involves access to and use of proprietary information must be extremely careful in how it conducts itself in the recruitment process. For example, a company should not target for recruitment an individual who is likely to have knowledge of the trade secrets of a competitor. It is a far better practice to have a formal job requisition prepared that is sufficiently detailed to identify the specific nature of the work to be performed but not so circumscribed as to limit its applicability to an individual in possession of competitors' trade secrets. The company should make a bona fide attempt to fill the position by resort to classified advertising and other methods routinely used in the industry to notify employees that a position is available. Moreover, the company should interview all interested candidates who are qualified even if the hoped-for candidate has indicated an interest, both in order to find the most highly qualified employee and to thwart the charge that the company was only interested in hiring away its competitor's trade secrets.

When a company learns of the imminent departure of an employee possessing knowledge of its proprietary information, it has available a number of measures for preventing the disclosure to or use of the proprietary information by others. It may well be appropriate, for example, to deny the employee continued access to proprietary materials. The employee might be requested to immediately return written materials pertaining to the company's processes or methods of operation. Certainly, the employee should be counseled as to what the company considers proprietary, and instructed as to what must not be taken from company premises. These matters are often handled during an exit interview, but a company would be well advised to consider addressing them as soon as it learns of the employee's plans, to avoid any misunderstanding in the interim.

By the same token, however, the prospective employer needs to take immediate steps to protect *its* own interests as soon as it has recruited an employee it believes may be claimed to have had access to proprietary information. The employee's existing employer may seek admissions as to the existence of trade secrets that the employee may not know how to respond to. For example, some high-technology lawyers counsel their clients to take an extremely aggressive posture vis-à-vis departing employees. They advise clients to extract written admissions from the employee to the effect that certain designated information constitutes the trade secrets or confidential business information of his employer, that the employer has taken adequate security measures to protect that information, that the information sought to be protected is not known outside of the company, that the employee has had access to designated items of information, and so forth. In a given instance, some of these sought-after admissions may not be true or may be only partly true, but the employee will be understandably confused as to how to respond. It is in the interest of the prospective employer to prevent the newly hired employee from making admissions that turn out later to be inaccurate, but which would prove to be an enormous embarrassment in any subsequent trade secret dispute. For this reason, a letter advising the newly hired employee to be wary is advisable. Here is a representative letter:

Dear Mr. Jones:

We are gratified that you have accepted employment with the Company, and we look forward to your arrival.

As you probably know, as long as your present employment continues you owe certain duties to your existing employer. We wish to draw your attention to some of these duties so that you do not overlook them. In particular, we want to call your attention to your obligation to protect the confidences of your present employer, if any. Like the Company, your present employer may possess proprietary information you have had access to. Such information should not be divulged to the Company, and we want you to be vigilant in this regard.

To avoid any misunderstandings, we also urge you not to take any documents, papers, notebooks, or the like with you when you leave unless you have obtained the prior written permission of your present employer. Even though you may not consider such materials to be proprietary, your present employer may disagree, and it would be the better practice to clear up the matter with your supervisor first. You should also inform your superiors of any item of equipment belonging to you and which you intend to remove from the premises.

(To be used in appropriate circumstances):

We would also like you to refrain from recruiting your colleagues or subordinates to join you. The Company may or may not have positions available for them, and in any event this practice is likely to arouse resentment on the part of your present employer. We realize that some of your colleagues may express an interest in joining you, in which case you may refer them to Mr. Franklin of our personnel office.

(To be used in appropriate curcumstances):

In the interim, it is also absolutely essential that you refrain from directly or indirectly soliciting business on behalf of the Company while you are employed with another firm. In fact, even notifying your existing clients and customers of your imminent change of employment might be misconstrued, so we think it advisable that you refrain from doing so until you have joined us. If customers or clients initiate the subject, you may inform them of your prospective employment, but we ask that you not engage in an extended conversation concerning your plans.

We also want to advise you of the practice at some companies of requesting a termination interview with employees for the purpose of extracting commitments from the departing employee concerning the protection of the company's proprietary information. Occasionally an employer may become overzealous in its efforts in this regard and may insist that the employee make oral or written acknowledgments which the employee may have no knowledge of, or may disagree with. Accordingly, we would appreciate it if you would give us as much advance notice as possible of any request by your present employer for a termination interview. We would also appreciate the opportunity to meet with you prior to such a termination interview, to decide whether an attorney should accompany you, and under what terms you should attend. Under no circumstances should you sign any agreement, understanding, or acknowledgment regarding your present employer's proprietary information before receiving the advice of counsel, and we request the opportunity to have our counsel review the contents of any such document before you sign it. If you do not know of any attorneys experienced in this area of the law, we can make some recommendations to you.

Please do not hesitate to contact me if you have any questions regarding the subject matter of this letter.

Very truly yours,

Obviously, such a letter need not be sent to every new recruit. There are only a few circumstances in which such a letter need be considered: (a) where a key employee is to be hired; (b) where the nature of the employee's prior responsibilities makes it likely that the employee possesses highly sensitive and confidential information; (c) where a communication from the existing employer indicates that a trade secret dispute may eventuate; (d) where the existing employer has a reputation for being litigious; (e) where the employee is in a position to influence colleagues and customers. But in an appropriate situation, the company should not hesitate to communicate its concerns to the new employee, both to warn him to be cautious and to establish in writing the company's instructions to avoid untoward conduct.

The penalty for failing to take such precautions can be severe. When one company in the plastics industry wanted to hire a technical employee from a competitor, it was shown a copy of the employee's confidentiality agreement and warned by the competitor's lawyer that the employee would be in breach of his agreement. The involvement of a lawyer was a certain sign of danger, and should have alerted the company to proceed with caution. Instead, the company, without even consulting its own attorney, told the employee the confidentiality agreement was not enforceable, agreed to indemnify him against legal expenses if he was sued, and proceeded to hire him, at a substantial increase in salary, to perform the same kind of work he had performed for his former employer. The result: the company was held to have induced the employee to breach his employment agreement, and not only was it held liable for $359,000 compensatory damages, but the judge also imposed $150,000 in punitive damages as well.

Another issue that requires attention at this juncture is whether to invoke the employee's prior education and experience as a rationale for employing him. To identify such factors as the motivating reason for employing a given individual tends to undermine a claim by the employee's previous employer that the rationale for his hiring was the appropriation of trade secrets. But documentation of this kind can bite back. If a trade secret dispute were to arise years later between the employee and the company, the company would be saddled with the admission that the employee had substantial relevant knowledge and experience before being employed by the company. As was indicated earlier, when a company hires individuals for the purpose of having the advantage of their prior knowledge and experience, the company is less likely to prevail in a suit asserting that information in the employee's possession is proprietary to the company and was obtained during the course of his employment.

The former employer may be so concerned about the prospect of its employee going to work for a competitor that it may feel compelled to notify the prospective employer of the nature of its proprietary claims. If this is done, it should be performed with circumspection and caution, but it should be done immediately, for if the subsequent employer innocently uses trade secrets misappropriated by the employee and in so doing expends substantial resources, it cannot be prevented from continuing to use the trade secrets. The communication should be made in writing so that it cannot be mischaracterized. Such a letter should not assert conclusions or inferences in the event they prove to be erroneous. It is quite adequate to put the subsequent employer on notice of a company's proprietary information claims by providing a copy of the employee's confidentiality agreement, a brief description of the employee's duties, and an enumeration of the categories of proprietary information to which the employee had access. These communications usually conclude with a request for assurance that the confidentiality of the company's proprietary information will be honored.

It is now the prospective employer's turn. Customarily, it will express shock and amazement that the classes of information enumerated could conceivably be regarded as proprietary. And while expressing its intention not to induce the newly hired employee to breach any confidence, it will request further details as to precisely what is claimed to be secret. The former employer will then send a reply which is marginally helpful. This sort of correspondence, which is usually conducted by company counsel, continues until each party is satisfied or has tired of the exchange.

In the majority of instances, the former employer will reach one of the following conclusions:

1. Its proprietary information is not so proprietary after all.
2. Its security procedures weren't so secure after all.
3. Its former employee didn't have access to the information, as first thought.
4. The information in dispute was already known to the employee before he commenced employment.
5. The information in dispute is already well known to the new employer.
6. The employee will not be employed in a capacity which puts the information at risk, and does not intend to disclose the information in violation of his fiduciary obligations.
7. The new employer does not intend to compete with respect to the product line to which the information relates.
8. The new employer, in recognition of its legal obligations, will not utilize the information, or seek its disclosure.
9. The information isn't valuable enough to get in a fight over.

During the course of the aforementioned volleys and returns, it is sometimes the case that one alleged trade secret is of foremost concern to the former employer. In order to avoid a lawsuit, the subsequent employer might consider agreeing to insulate the departing employee from use of that information and to independently develop the information through an outside consultant. Then no one can contend that the company violated its legal duties in employing the employee, or that the employee breached his fiduciary obligations and disclosed the information at issue to someone else. This strategy has been used to good effect by some companies. In one trade secret lawsuit against a start-up in the field of scientific instruments, the former employer was forced to concede that the only feature of the instrument at issue which it claimed to be confidential to it was the fact that they were microprocessor controlled; but the start-up had retained an outside consultant to provide the programming expertise!

While tiresome, these communications between former and new employers should be taken seriously, not only because they constitute a record that could someday find its way into court, but more significantly because most trade secret disputes can be nipped in the bud if the disputants take each other seriously and deal in good faith. Because of the potential cost, if even one lawsuit is averted over the course of many years, the effort expended in responding to the most spurious assertions will have been cost justified.

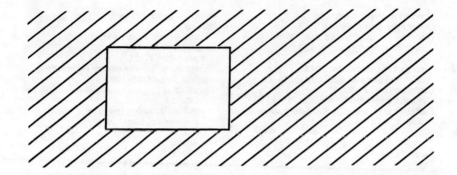

Index